Analects of Master Kuang-ch'in

Mu-ch'in Memorial Lecture Hall

Copyright c 1999 by Kuang-ch'in Cultural Foundation
Translated by Mu-ch'in Memorial Hall

Published by Mu-ch'in Memorial Hall

ISBN 957-97993-0-X (hardcover) ISBN 957-97993-1-8 (paperback)

in February 1999, First Edition, 2000 copies

Printed for free distribution by
The Corporate Body of the Buddha Educational Foundation
11F., 55 Hang Chow South Road Sec 1, Taipei, Taiwan, R.O.C.
Tel: 886-2-23951198 , Fax: 886-2-23913415
Email: overseas@budaedu.org
Website:http://www.budaedu.org

Master Kuang-ch'in (1892-1986) was born in Hui-an County of Fu-chien province in China. He was given up for adoption when he was four and was not educated, hence, illiterate.

He became a monk at the age of twenty-seven, but did not receive the formal bhiksu (monk) precepts until the age of forty-two. Mean-while, he practiced asceticism and recitation (of the name of Amitabha Buddha).

After receiving the full bhiksu precepts, he dwelled in a cave in the mountains where he practiced meditation alone for thirteen years and attained an elevated level. He came to Taiwan in 1947 and founded several monasteries, among them the Ch'eng-tien Temple of Taipei and Miao-tung Temple of Kao-hsiung. He had inspired a great many people into the dual practice of Zen and Pure Land doctrines.

Contents

Preface. vii

Translator's Note ix

1. On Practice. 001

2. On Keeping the Precepts. 063

3. On Reciting the Name of the Buddha. 069

4. On Reciting the Sutras. 091

5. On the Sense of Self 095

6. On Calming the Mind. 101

7. On Forbearance. 105

8. On Gossiping 111

9. On Work Ethics 117

10. On Habitual Patterns. 127

11. On a Simple Life. 131

12. On the Foul Body. 139

13. On the Pure Land 145

Preface

It has been more than a decade since Master Kuang-ch'in left us. Many continued to benefit from his teachings, thanks to his widely circulated analects. To make it more accessible to an even larger readership, a pocket-size version was published about six years ago. At the same time, I committed myself to the project of launching an English version so that my late Master's teachings can inspire Buddhists all over the world. While looking for a suitable translator, I first approached specialists at the foreign translation section of the *United Daily News.* They declined the task because, though the words are simple, the teachings of the Master are profound and by no means easy to convey in another language. While hosting a Buddhist summer camp for the children two years ago, I made the acquaintance of Dr. Amy R. Hwang of the Institute of Economies of the Academia Sinica. Dr. Hwang introduced me to Dr. Su-Ya Chang of the Institute of Modern History, also of the Academia Sinica, for the task. Professor Fei-chang Hwang of the English Department at the Chinese Cultural University kindly reviewed and made some suggestions to the manuscript.

This translation is based on a version published by the Yuanming Publisher. It was edited by the famous writer, Ms. Chien Chen, for the Miaotung Temple of Kaohsiung. Abbot Master Chuan-wen has generously given us permission to use it for this purpose. Published by the Kuang-ch'in Cultural and Educational Foundation and the Mu-ch'in Memorial Lecture Hall, this book will be printed in two versions: one in English only, the other with both English and Chinese texts. Both will be circulated abroad as well as in Taiwan. It is my greatest hope that upon reading and practicing the teachings of our great late Master, vexations of all sentient beings will gradually be lessened. On the eve of its publication, I am putting down a few words to record the process that brings about this volume and to express my appreciation to those who have helped along the way.

Chuan-yi, 1998

Translator's Note

The great late Master Kuang-ch'in received no formal education and was illiterate. Unlike many other contemporary Masters, he rarely gave public lectures and never wrote articles or exegeses of Buddhadharma. Collected in these analects are his verbal advice given to his disciples, mostly monastic practitioners in the temples where he was abbot.

As the Chinese version had to be edited for the sake of readability, its diction does already appear more sophisticated than the Master's own plain vernacular. Moreover, considering the likelihood that some of the ideas in this collection might prove difficult to understand for non-Chinese lay readers, I sometimes "interpret" the texts rather than translate verbatim. Thus, unfortunately, further fragments of the Master's original manner of speech had to be forfeited. However, no pains were spared to convey at least an inkling of its charming simplicity and animation. In view of my limited proficiency in both practice and the English language, it can only be hoped that the essence of these teachings has been rendered faithfully.

In the text, I have kept a few terms in Sanskrit. Instead of compiling a glossary, I gave their meanings in parentheses following the Sanskrit terms. Also, even though in practicing recitation, one may mindfully repeat the name of any buddha or bodhisattva, within this text, the name of the Buddha generally means "Amitabha Buddha."

In the process of translation, Professor Huang Fei-chang, my colleagues Ursula Ballin, Jiu-jung Luo, and my friends Lin Mei-chien and Cheryl Trusty have read either all or part of the manuscripts. Their useful comments have helped to make up some of my inadequacy, for which I am deeply grateful. Needless to say, all errors are mine, and mine alone.

I have benefited a great deal from the teachings of Master Kuang-ch'in through repeated pondering in the process of completing this work. It is my sincere hope that this book may be as beneficial to those who have a chance to read it as it is to myself.

Su-Ya Chang
December 3, 1998

.1.

On Practice

1   The negative karma we have accumulated in the eons has grown as high as a mountain. The purpose of practice is to eradicate such karma. If we fail to practice diligently and continue to create more negative karma, that mountain of obstruction will grow to ever more formidable height, barring us from escaping the cycle of birth and death.

2   Ascetic practice means cleansing our minds, or replacing the bad seeds within us: washing away the seeds of greed, anger, and ignorance common people cling to, replacing them by lovingkindness, compassion, sympathetic joy, and equanimity, which are the seeds of buddhahood and bodhisattvahood.

3   Ascetic practice is no easy matter! In our daily lives, we must train our minds to abstain from calculations and from discrimination. That is the essence of ascetic practice.

4   To practice, or be a practitioner, is easier said than done. As we are all subject to the common ailments of greed, anger, ignorance, pride, and doubt, let us carry out monastic duties with a purpose to train our minds and untie ourselves from such fetters. Only if we have attained that can we set out on the path of practice.

5   The purpose of practice is to eliminate our greed, anger, and ignorance so that our deeds, words, and thoughts will be pure and clean.

6   Wisdom will not unfold for those who do not eradicate their greed, anger, and ignorance.

7   Likewise, those who cling to the pleasure of the six *gunas* (sense objects, i.e. sight, sound, smell, taste, touch, and ideas) can not unfold their wisdom.

8   Most of the karma we are born with are negative, few are virtuous. Therefore, we must practice asceticism to eradicate our karmic obstructions.

9   Only after we have expelled evil thoughts can right mindfulness come to the fore and steer us away from *klesa* (vexations, i.e. attitudes, views, emotional states, or conditions, arising from

attachments, that cause suffering or dishar-
mony).

10 Asceticism is a great help in support of practice. Thus the great patriarchs and Bodhisattvas
Manjusri, Samantabhadra, Avalokitesvara, and
Ksitigarbha all took asceticism as their vow and
practice. Now, in our practice, we ought to
follow their determination, treading the paths
of the bodhisattvas.

11 When Master Hsu Yun set out on his pilgrimage,
he left bare-footed, took along only a stool and a
simple bundle, and passed many a day with
scanty food. He would just follow his path,
never worrying about the next day. Since his
mind was free of clinging, all the dragon kings
and *devas* safeguarding the Dharma protected
and maintained him. We simply lack such determination; or else there should be nothing we
might not accomplish in our practice.

12 "Wild cranes seek no fodder: the wide world is
theirs." They fly and rest as they please and are
truly "free." Our practice ought to be like that:
tranquil wherever we are, free and easy
whether at rest or in action. Come what may,
our minds should remain still and unmoved.
Such is the state of *"samadhi* (perfect absorption)."

13   Expect and embrace obstacles! For without them, we can not make progress in our practice. Only when we comprehend the true nature of adversity and be free of vexations would our wisdom unfold. For example, when provoked by someone, our minds nevertheless remain tranquil, calm, and free of vexations. That is the essence of practice.

14   Practice means "doing what others won't;" only in this way will we be able to eradicate karma and raise merit. Therefore, we should vow to practice diligently. Let us not argue with others and refuse to take up tasks because "That matter is no concern of mine," bickering as worldly persons are wont to do. Practitioners do not haggle, do not calculate how much work "they" have done as opposed to "I." Such behavior undermines practice and would not facilitate the advance of merit and wisdom.

15   Practice aims at retrieving our true nature: "that certain state" in which we were before we were born. You fail to understand this now because your wisdom has not yet unfolded. It is like the moon veiled by dark clouds: its true nature, although shining, can not be seen.

16 Practitioners should not quibble over who is right or wrong. When accused of being in the wrong, accept it even though you know you are right. If you are ready to admit mistakes, you will remain untroubled; if not, your mind will be disturbed and vexation will follow.

17 Ascetic practice means training yourself to "renounce your body" (i.e. renouncing physical desires and cravings). You should realize that no matter how well you take care of it, this body is unreal and will eventually decay. What does it mean when we speak of "renouncing the body?" It means to dress unobtrusively, to eat plain fare, and in general to live a moderate life. Stop craving for lavish clothes, meals, and living conditions is the first step into practice.

18 The harder the path of practice, the closer to enlightenment you will be. Do not expect people to treat you well, otherwise you shall be no different from a lay person.

19 Learn to take losses or be taken advantage of without resentment. Strive to be tolerant rather than calculating so that you may progress in practice.

20 "Keep constant watch over our own transgressions, and we will not stray from the right path."
The more we practice, the easier it will become
for us to discover our own shortcomings and
feel remorse.

21 Practice to remain tranquil and unfettered
whether in action or at rest. What does this
mean? It means that while you are active, your
mind should stay calm and unswayed by your
concerns; but while you are at rest, you must
not cling to the idea, or to the appearance, of
"motionlessness."

22 "Sweep the dust by reciting the name of
(Amitabha) Buddha, and the Lotus will flourish." This stanza means that we practitioners
ought to be guided by right mindfulness, purify
our minds and turn all evil thoughts into proper
ones by incessant recital of the Buddha's name.

23 Take everything as it comes; nothing ought to
disturb the mind of a practitioner. Forgo your
cravings for worldly goods such as lavish
clothes, meals, housing, cars, as well as all your
sense of judgment, praise, or blame. Once you
have untied yourself from physical and mental
distractions, wisdom will unfold. Conduct your
daily lives in an unobtrusive fashion--the path

is the wisdom of ordinariness. Also, abstain from both vexation and exultation. Treat others neither overly kind nor too harsh. Foster good karmic affinity with others when occasions arise but do not court their favor. Be forever on the watch over your own thoughts and take note whenever an evil notion arises.

24 The only way to grasp the essence of the Dharma is to practice in person. Once you have truly understood the bitter misery of both living in this world and the perpetual wondering through the cycle of rebirths, your wisdom will unfold. Increasing awareness will then lead you on to the path of supreme enlightenment.

25 Once you have obtained wisdom through practice, your mind will become clear and keen, and you shall be able to complete all your tasks satisfactorily and without obstacles. Therefore, to deliver other beings, you must first liberate yourself lest you should lead them astray. Then, people will more readily accept your teaching.

26 Practice requires perseverance; do not aspire to any instant enlightenment. Without reciting the name of the Buddha continuously thereby removing omnipresent illusions, how can you hope for any attainment? But if you exercise

faith, dedication, and practice reciting the name of the Buddha continuously, even during your daily round, you will quite naturally arrive at an enlightened mind and at the realization of the buddha-nature immanent in all beings.

27 Come what may: the mind of a practitioner ought to remain calm, unfettered, and unobstructed. Indeed, it is at the attainment of such "complete freedom" that our practice aims.

28 In order to attain true comprehension of the Dharma, you must practice yourself. Just as they say, "He who drank it knows whether the water was cold or warm." Go ahead and practice yourself; only then may you have genuine attainment.

29 Emulate the good (examples given by others), ignore the bad. Keep your sense of right and wrong to yourself. Unpleasant circumstances are propitious for the practice of forbearance. Practice is not about judging who is right or wrong or who has more reason. Rather, the strength of practice lies on whether you can remain undisturbed under challenge.

30 It may come to pass that the master blames you for not having swept the floor even after you

have indeed done so. If you object, debating right and wrong, you will not yet be in any way different from a lay person. If, however, you accept the reproach, answering, "Fine, I shall sweep it again," you have set out into practice.

31 "Forbearance" is fundamental to practice. If you forbear with others, you will be able to reform people wherever you go because forbearance brings forth moral conduct and forestalls resentment. As people enjoy your company, you will quite naturally attract them toward practice.

32 Practice forbearance! This is the root and foundation of our practice. If you lack forbearance, you are a monastic practitioner in name only. Therefore, do not presume that you are right in whatever you do. If you don't abstain from seeing everything your "own way," you can never practice forbearance.

33 Practice means looking inward and gain awareness of your own mind, not going after matters of the outward world. Instead of tying your happiness solely on agreeable circumstances, your mind should naturally be filled with dharmic joy from practice. Guard yourself against capriciousness and indecision lest your

mind should come under the sway of external conditions. If you can abstain from attachment to the form and sense of "self," you are honestly treading the path of practice.

34 In your practice, strive to personify lovingkindness and compassion. This must radiate from the expression in your eyes and let people sense that here, indeed, is a kind, compassionate person. Only then will you be able to summon people toward faith in the Buddha, learning and practicing Buddhadharma.

35 In group practice, if one attains a certain level, all others benefit. They will be inspired to follow his/her example and practice vigorously. Since all of you wish to practice and karmic affinity has brought you together, you ought to help and encourage each other along the way. If, however, you allow sentiments of judgment, jealousy, and delusion to flourish, it will not only affect your companions' resolution but will also impede your own tranquility in practice.

36 Practice aims at unfolding wisdom, but you ought to cultivate merit as well. Be forever merciful and compassionate, try your best to help those in need and foster good karmic affinity with others. This, then, is the dual practice toward gaining both merit and wisdom.

37 Set out with the dual practice toward gaining merit and wisdom. As you get on in life, gradually attaining both, you will quite naturally reach the ultimate goal of practice.

38 Be merciful to all beings. Remember that they, like us, were born into this world so as to practice and plant good seeds. Therefore, be merciful and compassionate. Tread the bodhisattva-path and wish that: "May all beings, sentient or otherwise, acquire buddha-wisdom."

39 Worshipers bring offerings to the temple with the intention of seeking merit. You must not assess these offerings at their material value. Whatever is offered, if only a blade of grass, we should accept with joy. Most important of all: do not distinguish the offerings; for as soon as you do, you would desire the good ones and despise the bad. You might become vexed or even create negative karma through sneering at them hence spoil your practice. Handle the offerings as they come, use your wisdom to make the best out of them. Such will then be in keeping with the dual practice toward attaining merit and wisdom.

40 Those who wish to tread the bodhisattva-path must never think, "As long as I myself am doing

fine, what are the others to me?" It is indeed the others whose welfare should always be foremost on your mind--even at your own expenses. On the other hand, if you only look after your own concerns, endless delusive vexations will follow.

41 Monastic practitioners ought to be kind and compassionate to all beings while providing them with expedient guidance for practice. Remember, all bodhi fruits grow out of lovingkindness and compassion.

42 After I am gone, there is no need to worry that no one would guide you in your practice. Just remember what I told you: reciting the name of the Buddha; practice diligently and with firm determination; abstain from the pleasures of the six senses; adapt yourselves to circum- stances (rather than insisting on your own way). If you are able to do so, it will be as if I were still among you.

43 You might enjoy a great deal listening to your Master's expositions and feel them quite agree- able. However, such "agreeableness" reflects the stage reached by your Master. As for your own level of attainment, it depends on how much you put those teachings into practice. Only through such a process will you be able to fully

comprehend and verify their truthfulness and usefulness.

44 True listening does not rest in how much you have listened to your Master but in how well you have listened. Even if you have listened well, you would benefit only if you can apply properly what you have heard to the circum-stances you come across.

45 We who chose the path of ascetic practice ought to regard all circumstances and hardships as good opportunities to discipline our minds and bodies. Such training will help to cut off our delusion and vexations, to cleanse our habitual patterns, and to toughen us against all resis-tance. Merely performing laborious tasks in the temple certainly does not turn us into ascetics. Therefore, you who have left home for practice ought not to be afraid of hardships. Only through overcoming continuous adversities can we discipline our minds and unfold our wis-dom.

46 "Without hardships, there can be no attainment in practice." Walking the path of asceticism requires firm determination. With such will-power, you naturally will not discriminate against tasks assigned to you. Instead, you will

carry them out devotedly without even considering them as menial, for such tasks will wear
down your pride and help to reduce your karmic obstructions. Therefore, a practitioner
ought not to be afraid of, nor try to escape from,
hardships, for without them there is nothing to
practice on hence no attainment to speak of.

47 There are eight kinds of misery from which we
constantly suffer: birth, aging, disease, death,
separation from loved ones, company of hated
ones, failure to obtain what we desire, and all
the ills of the five *skandhas* (form, sensation,
perception, volition, and consciousness). In
addition, we are also vexed by our greed, anger,
and ignorance. Unenlightened as we are, we
totter from day to day under the full sway of
such delusive and afflictive karma, suffering
immensely. Without diligent practice under the
guidance of Buddhadharma, we can never be
liberated.

48 Among the four forms of birth, the spiritual
level of human beings is the most elevated.
However, if we do not understand the Dharma
and the principle of causality, we might kill
animals just to satisfy our desires of eating
meat. This will create very severe karmic
obstructions. Listen! As we butcher those crea-

tures, they, too, know the pangs of death and
will scream out miserably, and those are
screams of resentment. If we kill them anyway,
we shall come under the sway of this negative
karmic affinity. This will start a vicious cycle of
killing and revenge, barring us forever from
escaping samsara. For this reason, a Buddhist
should faithfully keep the precept against killing, cultivating a compassionate mind instead.

49 Among the six divisions, our human existence is
by no means easy to attain! The idea, though, is
that we should grasp this unique opportunity
for practice so as to break out the cycle of birth
and death and ultimately reach buddhahood. Do
not accumulate additional negative karma
through our greed, anger, ignorance, and endless pursuits of tasty food, lavish clothing,
worldly pleasures, children and grandchildren,
etc. If, instead of diligent practice, we remain
attached to the six sensual objects and lose this
precious opportunity of human existence, we
will be forever confined to samsara. Be aware
that human beings can easily be reborn as animals like cows, horses, pigs, dogs, etc., hell-
beings, or hungry ghosts. Where we end up
depends on where we put our minds. We can
either utilize this human existence to practice
in the hope of attaining buddhahood, or to

create more negative karma hence confine ourselves in the six divisions of rebirth. Since we all have chosen to leave home for practice, wouldn't it be wise for us to follow the Dharma and find a suitable way to escape the entanglement and torment of samsara?

50 When leaving home for practice, both your body and your mind should "leave." In other words, genuine renunciation means you ought to have as little secular entanglement as possible. In case your parents or relatives come for a visit, discuss with them only Buddhadharma so as to convert and deliver them. Do not indulge in the sentiment of parting from loved ones. Otherwise, you will be a monastic practitioner in name only. And such attachment will surely become a great impediment to your practice and to your attainment of total liberation.

51 Relinquish all aspirations to secular gains! Not only must we part with our greed for wealth, but likewise with our hankering after fame. In fact, there is nothing in this world with which we should be reluctant to part. We monastic practitioners should go even further: consuming only plain food and clothing, devoting ourselves to our tasks in the monastery for the benefit of all beings, and keeping our minds

solely on practice. Only through such ascetic practice can we eradicate our karmic obstructions and free our minds of illusive ideas as well as other disturbances. If we live our lives, day in day out, in this manner, we are truly treading the path of practice.

52 The essence of practice is to train the mind. How, then, shall we proceed? First, train our minds to abstain from discrimination, attachment, and vexations. Most people, not realizing this principle, are prone to distinguish good and evil, right and wrong, love and distaste. Practitioners, on the other hand, ought to abstain from discriminating what we see or hear, not to become attached to, or vexed by, them. Such is the practice of training the mind. If a monastic practitioner carries on the habit of gossiping around and judging people, then he/she is a monastic practitioner in name only. Such behaviors are not in tune with the Dharma; in fact, they only reflect the impurity of our eyes and ears. Such "discrimination," though involuntary, will nevertheless defile our minds, create vexation, and lead us astray from the path of liberation.

53 Do not anticipate any specific form through which bodhisattvas deliver sentient beings. The

process (of deliverance) often occurs quietly and naturally. Whether sentient beings can be delivered depends on the degree of their faith, resolution, and willingness to take refuge in the bodhisattvas. While the compassion of bodhisattvas to deliver is the primary cause, deliverance can not take place without the secondary cause, i.e. the vow and dedication of those who wish to be delivered. In other words, only when the two causes correspond will deliverance be possible. Take Bodhisattva Avalokitesvara (Kuanyin) for example. Sitting high up on the altar, the Bodhisattva appears to be motionless. However, her compassion and mercifulness have been providing relief to many who prayed for help and, in response to their faith, guiding them through the practice of the Dharma.

54 Instead of chattering on worldly matters, we monastic practitioners ought to discuss only about the Dharma. Otherwise, how can there be any "practice" to speak of if we carry on the discriminating, calculating, and competitive demeanor and gossip like lay people do?

55 Most parents wish for their children to grow up to have a bright future: college education, doctoral degree, wealth and success, etc. Unfortunately, many turn their backs on their

parents after attaining success. But these parents, failing to realize its futility, continue to place their hope on their children. For many, their concern of, hence attachment to, their children and grandchildren would never cease, not even to the moment of their last breath. They do not realize that such deep affection will confine them to the six divisions of rebirth. Their expectations, attachments, and concerns are the very cause of their lingering in samsara, hence the sources of their perpetual misery.

56 Buddhists believe that "Craving for just a blade of grass, and it will guarantee your remaining in samsara." A blade of grass stands for an object of this world, and desire of which will result in your rebirth into it. A blade of grass also represents a thought, and possession of which will prevent you from transcending the three realms of sentient existence. Even if the object you desire or the thought you have is as trivial as a blade of grass, it is nevertheless powerful enough to confine you in the cycle of birth and death.

57 Regard everything you come across as a blessed reward and conserve it mindfully. Do not squander anything edible or useful; rather, use your wit and patience in handling things broken

or worn. Put your mind into it, then you will set out into the dual practice of gaining both merit and wisdom.

58 "Before attaining buddhahood, be sure to foster good karmic affinity with people." As practitioners, we ought to help others the best we can, be patient and not calculating, joyfully foster good affinity with all beings--even with an evil person or an animal. If, unfortunately, you sense that people don't really like you or feel unpleasant seeing you, it is because you did not foster good affinity with them in previous lives. Therefore, be sure to foster good relations with everyone so that you may later enjoy blessed rewards and favorable affinities. By then, you will have the good karmic conditions necessary to deliver other sentient beings.

59 How magnanimous and merciful Maitreya Buddha and Putai Hoshang (Cloth-bag Monk) are! If we can not emulate them, i.e. we would take no losses, nor tolerate any criticism, then we have not attained any level in our practice!

60 If a practitioner does not practice diligently, does not work for the benefit of others, does not accumulate merits, does not keep his precepts, practice meditation, or foster the growth of

wisdom, then the dragon kings and *devas* safe-guarding the Dharma will not watch over him. He will then be under the full sway of his karmic obstructions and all sorts of problem will arise. On the other hand, if he keeps himself well and practices attentively, all *devas* will come to his protection. With the mind pure and free, he will then be able to practice without distraction.

61 What does it mean when we say that someone looks solemn and dignified? When one does not act upon ignorance and delusion, when one constantly purifies one's body and mind, he/she will acquire a natural solemn and dignified manner. When one enacts the ideas of lovingkindness, compassion, sympathetic joy and equanimity, when one conducts him/herself in good manners, he/she will look solemn and dignified.

62 We practitioners should dedicate ourselves to "attain buddhahood and deliver all sentient beings." However, we must work on our own salvation first so that we may acquire the ability to deliver others. The first step is to forgo our desire to eat, dress, and live lavishly, and to forsake our secular affections, attachments, and our incessant pursuit of wealth and fame. Only when our mind

and bodies become pure and free of hindrance can we begin to talk about preaching Buddhadharma for the benefit of all sentient beings. Otherwise, with our own minds enslaved by secular attachments, how can we help to free others from such bondage?

63 As practitioners, we ought to relinquish all cravings for good food, nice clothing, comfortable housing, wealth and fame, etc. In other words, we can begin our practice by curbing desires stimulated by what we see, hear, smell, taste, touch, and think, thereby shake off the fetters of sensual passions. This is how the strength of our practice may grow. Therefore, we monastic practitioners ought to content ourselves with a simple life and really devote ourselves to practice. Only by so doing can we hope to win the confidence and respect of all beings and become genuine masters who, while liberating ourselves, can guide them out of their misery.

64 We ought to recognize that "Only through endurance can we transcend hardships, and only through forbearance can we gain blessed rewards." The amount of karmic obstructions we can reduce is proportional to the hardships we endure and the efforts we put into practice. Similarly, merits can only be earned through diligent practice, not external pursuits.

65 Do understand that sitting meditation does not mean sitting there idly, doing nothing. Most important of all, do not cling to the ideas that "I am meditating," "I am reciting the name of the Buddha," or "I am practicing Zen," otherwise, you will be practicing with the omnipresence of the sense of "self." If you continue to dwell on the idea that "I am doing this and that," you are still clinging to erroneous and illusive thoughts and can never be genuinely free. In this way, even if you meditate for thousands of years, the effect will be the same as cooking rocks or steaming sands--all useless in terms of getting yourself to transcend the cycle of birth and death. Forsake all forms, attach your mind to nothing, and think not of what you are doing. Also, conduct your daily activities (be it moving, staying, sitting, or sleeping) without clinging to any idea of purity, or dwell on any dharma. Only by steering clear of all discrimination and differentiation can you transcend the three realms and break out of the prison of samsara.

66 Real life is very much like a soap opera in which everyone plays a role. We all have the experience of following the emotional swings of the characters of soap operas. However, we rarely sense that the ensuing sentiments of joy, anger, sorrow, and happiness are but distinctions made by our own

minds. It is much the same in real life. More often than not, we allow our distinction of circumstances or judgments of people to take charge of our emotions without even being conscious about it. Furthermore, it seems that we always find it easier to emulate bad examples than good ones. This is because our delusions accumulated through the eons can easily overwhelm us. Hence, we are often swayed by circumstances befitting our sinister desires. On the other hand, how often have we claimed that "to tolerate the intolerable and practice the impracticable" is the attainment of buddhas and bodhisattvas, thereby excusing ourselves for not following their examples but merely praising them with empty words? The most unfortunate result is that we keep on ingraining bad habits while shunning the good. This is what we called the misconception of an ordinary person, and it is due largely to our lack of firm resolve (to practice).

67 Many people, having no real understanding of Buddhadharma, are apt to comment that monks and nuns are no different from the laity: they get sick, run into troubles, and will eventually die. What they do not recognize is that even though disease and calamity attack monastic practitioners as they do ordinary people, the degree of spiritual enlightenment of the former is immensely different

from that of the latter. Ordinary people, with an unenlightened mind, suffer gravely and complain bitterly upon misfortune; when they die, they are driven by karmic forces and continue to roam among the four forms of birth. When practitioners pass away, however, they would readily forsake their karmic-driven bodies and, guided by their inner light to transcend the six divisions of rebirth, go straight to the Pure Land.

68 The reason that some people are affluent and prestigious is because they have accumulated a great deal of merits through generous giving in previous lives. However, there is a catch taking pleasure from such rewards. Without suffering from impermanence and all sorts of frustration, people may easily indulge in them, unaware of the need, nor searching for the means, to escape the prison of samsara. When time comes that they have used up all their rewards, they will be driven by other karmic forces and continue to roam in the eternal cycle of rebirths.

69 Keep reminding ourselves that we are practicing for the benefit of all beings, and this will in turn bring us immeasurable rewards. Only by so doing can we transcend the captivity of discrimination between self and others, and let go all our attachments, inverted dreams, as well as our greed,

anger, and ignorance, etc. We can also gradually be free of the vexations caused by the attachment to "the form of self," and the infinite *samadhi* of our true nature will then unfold. Therefore, the premise of our practice should always be for the benefit of others, and the foundation the deliverance of all beings. Only then can we expand the horizon of our concern and attain genuine liberation.

70 We monastic practitioners ought not to have fear of adverse circumstances, for it is exactly those "baffled, confounded, unfitting, and uncomfortable" conditions that we practice to tackle. These adverse courses will help, along our way of practice, to unfold our wisdom, enhance our tolerance, and gradually free us from all fetters. And as our wisdom develops to a certain level, we would naturally overcome vexations of that level. Therefore, those who really know how to practice never feel apprehensive about adverse circumstances.

71 Ascetic practice means to train our minds through our daily chores about the temple. In carrying out our tasks, we should learn to bear hardships and extend the level of our tolerance. After a while, we may find the tasks less unbearable, indicating the waning of our karmic obstructions. On the other

hand, if we feel growing pain and impatience, we are under the full swing of our karmic obstructions. As we know, buddhas and bodhisattvas, with all their karmic obstructions eradicated through ascetic practice, are free of vexations and pain. They have attained perfect freedom hence having no sense that they are "doing something" or "delivering sentient beings."

72 The sun does not discriminate: it shines on virtuous people as well as on immoral ones. This is how we should treat others. The morality of others is their concern only; we ought to treat everyone with similar compassion and lovingkindness. If we discriminate against some people because they are immoral, then we are not that much different from them.

73 When carrying out our daily tasks about the temple, do not feel that we are doing it for the buddhas, the bodhisattvas, or the Master. In fact, we are doing it solely for the reduction of our own karmic obstructions. As I often tell you "There isn't much to learn here; all I do is asking you to sweep the floor and do other laborious chores." However, do not think floor-sweeping is an easy matter. If not doing it right, you may feel vexed and come under the sway of your delusive karma. Therefore, not only should you sweep the floor clean, but also

do it gladly: feel that you are at the same time
sweeping away all delusive vexations, all obstructions of arrogance, envy, and ignorance, and all
dusts clouding your wisdom, and, while doing this,
fill your mind with dharmic joy. Were you able to
do so, you can claim that you truly know how to
sweep the floor. Practice, then, means mindfully
carrying out daily tasks and, through which, eliminating all vexations so as to break out of the cycle
of birth and death.

74　The key to practice is the mind. When the mind is
pure, there shall be no hindrance on the path of
practice. Likewise, the key to deliverance of all
beings is also the "mind." When attempting to
deliver others, put your mind into it but do not be
forceful, selective, or discriminating. Whatever
forms or shapes beings take, be they rich or poor,
smart or dumb, help and guide them just the same.
Moreover, do not attach to the sense that "I am
delivering these sentient beings!"

75　Your practice will be enhanced by the realization
that you are but an ordinary person. It makes you
humble hence more willing to embrace teachings
of masters and practice diligently. Otherwise, you
might be too arrogant to learn and, consequently,
unwilling to practice. Practice means to walk the
path step by step, to adjust and discipline your

mind through challenges. Only when your mind becomes its own master, free of all delusions and vexations, unsusceptible to the swing of circum- stances, can there be hope for any attainment in practice. Therefore, practice should begin with the training of "your own mind," which no one else can do for you. If you practice to the extent that your mind is free of all fetters, your intrinsic nature will manifest and wisdom unfold.

76　Ascetic practice is the best way to expel erroneous and illusive thoughts. When facing impossible and unbearable circumstances, let go of all aspirations and attachments and practice with an undivided mind. With our minds gradually free of discrimi- nation and vexations, our karmic obstructions and delusions will naturally be reduced and our hearts filled with dharmic joy. Keep on such practice and the degree of our awareness will grow and our wisdom unfold. By then, everything will become crystal clear thus easily comprehensible.

77　It is clear in Buddhist history that the great patri- archs always kept a low profile and pursued no fame. As we know, those who desire less of worldly fame and gains are more apt to practice diligently. Too many secular concerns distract our minds and make us pretentious. Under these circumstances, no attainment is possible and our efforts of leaving home for practice will all be in vain.

78 Wisdom is much more powerful than supernatural
capability, for the latter is but the ingenious appli-
cation of the former. Wisdom is the inner light
that enables us to discern and comprehend the
essence of everything; it helps us eliminate all
vexations generated by our ignorance and escape
the cycle of birth and death. Therefore, if you
covet supernatural capability rather than wisdom,
you will have no hope of attaining buddhahood.
Instead, you will remain in the three realms and
be confined to the six divisions of rebirth.

79 The purpose of practice is not for others to see.
Ostentatious practice gains no strength and lack of
substance, and will be easily detected by others. As
the *Diamond Sutra* puts it: "No bodhisattva who
is a real bodhisattva distinguishes forms of self, of
others, of sentient beings, and of life." Therefore,
practice is a very "private" business. It is a training
of your own mind to introspect the incipience and
motivation of your each and every thought, which
can never be attained through external pursuits.
Even if you have attained a certain stage, do not
show off lest it should hamper your practice.

80 Genuine practitioners ought to have firm "faith"
and strong "resolve." The harder the situations
become, the deeper their understanding of the
Dharma will be hence the stronger their persever-

ance in practice. That is why "no attainment is possible without hardship." Monastic practitioners should expect a lifestyle vastly different from that of laity, and realize that, the more arduous the circumstances are, the better for practice.

81 Unlike the laity, practitioners should not argue about right or wrong. Once there were two disciples practicing meditation. One sat in a very solemn and dignified manner, the other quite at ease, not even keeping his posture. However, the master hit the former with incense board to test whether his mind was as solemn and dignified as his posture indicated. If not, he would resent the master and become vexed. On the other hand, if his mind were solemn and dignified, he would humbly request the instruction of the master to improve his practice. So, as you see, instead of quibbling over right and wrong, what you really should do is constantly introspecting whether you yourself have gained genuine strength through practice. Here is a good measurement of strength: when others insist you are wrong even though you have done everything correctly, you can sincerely accept such criticism.

82 When leaving home for practice, be sure to select a large monastery. The experience of living together with more people provides ample opportunities to

practice against diverse circumstances. When practitioners live in a small group without the restraint of monastic rules, they may easily indulge themselves hence forfeit the opportunities to discipline and train their minds.

83 It may be inevitable that, in the secular world, people are classified as rich or poor, prestigious or humble; however, there should be no such distinctions among Buddhists. Whatever people's financial or social status may be, you ought to treat them equally and with similar lovingkindness and compassion. "Before attaining buddhahood, be sure to foster good karmic affinity with all people." Only by fostering good relations with as many sentient beings as possible will you create the dharmic affinity to deliver them in the future.

84 Be sure to contemplate thoroughly about the meaning of the "Three Refuges." For instance, we take refuge in the Dharma where "wisdom is as immeasurable as the sea." What is "wisdom?" According to Buddhadharma, the nature of wisdom is "emptiness," and it can only be developed through practice, not thinking. Furthermore, wisdom has neither form nor color, so there is no concrete object that can be called "wisdom." The teachings of the Buddha, as recorded in the sutras, represent "wisdom." If we can manage everything in our daily

lives satisfactorily without generating vexations, such is wisdom at work.

85 We know that there are all sorts of "situations" or "circumstances," but where do they come from? They originate from the distinction in our minds. Make no distinction, then no circumstance exists.

86 It is a great agony that we are now all confined to the cycle of birth and death, transmigrating among the six divisions of sentient existence. Indeed, life is tough. However, it is only through rebirths and practice as human beings that we can hope to attain buddhahood; no practice is possible without this ordeal. Our suffering enables us to appreciate more the pain of all beings hence helps to strengthen our resolve to tread the bodhisattva-path and practice myriad methods of the six *paramitas* (giving, ethics, forbearance, diligence, meditation, and wisdom). With compassion and forbearance, we can advance ourselves while benefiting others. And via the ordeal of samsara, we can accumulate merits for our ultimate liberation and supreme enlightenment.

87 How can we attain right mindfulness in practice? We can start by simplifying our demands for food, clothing, and living conditions. Do not desire or be attached to material comforts, nor make distinc-

tions about their qualities as long as they are sufficient to sustain our lives. This might sound easy, but is by no means easy to carry out. We must practice vigorously to eliminate avarice, which in turn will bring forth right mindfulness. Then, when our time in this world is up, we can avoid the distractions of inverted ideas and be guided by our inner light.

88 If you choose to practice in the monastery, there is a basic requirement, i.e., you should desire no lavish food, clothing, and living conditions, just live on whatever is available. This is what we call "to be sustained by the nature." And because you take whatever comes to you, greediness will not arise.

89 Some people, though practicing vigorously, deviate from the path because they remain attached to the "forms" of self, others, sentient beings, and life, which only induce vexations and inverted ideas. These people might claim to have attained a certain stage, but in fact are unknowingly treading the wrong path. Worse, they might lead others astray. This deviation results from a lack of correct understanding of Buddhadharma.

90 Monastic practitioners ought to avoid distractions. Practice for the sake of practice itself so as to

strengthen your resolve and stabilize your mind. Do not plan on being uneventful and be prepared to endure hardships--not just of laborious tasks, but of all kinds of challenges. Hardships and vexations are tests of your strength. Use your wisdom to subdue impediments of the mind and your determination to overcome all difficulties. "Adverse circumstances are good for practice. Without them no progress will be made toward ultimate liberation."

91   The Old Master practiced reciting the name of the Buddha all his life. When he first became a monk, Master Chuan-chen, the abbot of the temple, recognized his potential and taught him this method. Once, another Master was expounding the sutras in the temple, the Old Master wished to attend. Master Chuan-chen nevertheless said to him: "Why listen? Go recite the name of the Buddha and carry on your ascetic practice!" The Old Master was upset, thinking: "The purpose of becoming a monk is to learn the sutras. Now the Master would not even let me listen!" However, the moment he realized what went through his mind, he changed his perception and said: "I will do whatever the Grand Master has told me to." So the Old Master continued his ascetic practice and reciting the Buddha's name, accumulating both merit and wisdom. In this way, he was able to

attain an exalted stage in practice. Therefore, he taught us to concentrate on reciting the name of the Buddha as he did himself. The doctrine of the Pure Land is the most direct and secure one among all disciplines; it also is the most suitable method for contemporary people.

92 The *Heart Sutra* describes the practice of Bodhisattva Avalokitesvara, "Kuan-Tzu-Chai," the Sovereign Regarder. What does "Tzu-Chai" mean? It means reflecting on the mind so that it will attain "perfect freedom." Whatever circumstances emerge, or whenever illusive thoughts arise, the mind should remain tranquil. Continue to recite the name of the Buddha while making no distinction between, nor even think of the idea of, "good" and "bad." Do not feel "happy" or "agitated," just keep a watchful eye on your own mind. Such is the state of "Kuan-Tzu-Chai." But being introspective does not mean that you should keep pondering: "how is it?" Rather, just be alert and take note of illusive thoughts or evil ideas at their incipience, lest they should take control of your mind. Such practice will ensure that your mind is "free" and "pure" at all times. Wherever you are and whatever you do, be it reciting the name of the Buddha or performing prostration, within or outside of the temple, if your mind is free of the sway of circumstances, you have attained the state of "Kuan-Tzu-Chai."

93   All methods of practice as taught by the Buddha focus on the mind; when we practice, we are also learning how to discipline our minds. A well-composed mind resembles clear and placid water that truthfully reflects whatever appears above it. Likewise, when our minds attain absolute tranquility, we will be able to grasp the essence of everything. The purpose of reciting the name of the Buddha is to help still our minds so that they may be as pure and tranquil as placid water. A restless and scattered mind resembles muddy water from which evil and discriminatory ideas easily arise. When our minds are in such a state, we are prone to make distinctions of what we see, hear, smell, taste, touch, and think, thereby indulge in the pursuit of sensual passions. Therefore, we must recite the name of the Buddha to the extent that our minds become absolutely clear and pure, neither defiled by nor attached to sense objects. When we reach that stage, naturally we will not cling to the five *skandhas* (form, sensation, perception, volition, and consciousness). With our six organs untainted by the six causes of impurity, we can truly realize the emptiness of the five *skandhas* thus be free of all vexations. Then, we can naturally help to relieve all sentient beings from their misery. And with the essence of our minds enlightened and our wisdom unfolded, we can easily comprehend even the most abstruse part of Buddhadharma.

94 We chose to leave home for practice so that we may concentrate on eliminating our physical and psychological desires. However, do not become attached to any particular ascetic method. For example, some insist on giving up food and sleep, which might result in a physical disorder causing mental and/or physical aberrations and weak-nesses. In the end, they might not be able to eat or sleep at all. Under the circumstances, they can easily go astray if they have yet to attain right mindfulness. Therefore, do not insist on, or be attached to, the method of "no food, no sleep," or to any specific austerity. After all, it is necessary to sustain this physical body so that we may continue our practice. What we should do is not to stray from ordinariness; adopt a "middle way" in our daily activities so as to maintain our physical as well as mental strength. This middle way will sustain us in the long path of practice and help us avoid unnecessary hindrances.

95 How can we be Buddhists? Just take refuge in the Buddha, the Dharma, and the *Sangha.* The *Triratna* (Three Jewels) are an integral whole: without Buddha, there will be no Dharma, without Dharma, no Sangha. What, then, is Dharma? Dharma represents the truth realized by the Buddha. It is what the Buddha learned from his practice and he taught it to us for our salvation.

We can practice according to the Dharma to attain enlightenment. As we know, "Those unenlightened are ordinary beings; the enlightened ones are buddhas." If we constantly keep our minds in the state of reciting the name of the Buddha, we will be "enlightened" therefore are "buddhas." In other words, if each and every thought of ours is a recitation of the Buddha's name, then we are constantly in the state of "enlightenment."

96 For eons, we have been roaming through the cycle of birth and death. Despite this life's human existence, we remain in the six divisions of rebirth with all vicious ideas and evil seeds accumulated through the eons following us like shadows. Hence, we must repent unremittingly for our past karmic obstructions. This is exactly what we should do when we receive our precepts because it is the only way we can attain pure and clean precepts. Indeed, with buddha-nature immanent in all beings, it nevertheless takes diligent practice and sincere repentance to attain buddhahood.

97 What makes a monastery invaluable is its strict discipline imposed on all its members. Therefore, as soon as you enter the monastery, you should act according to the monastic, rather than secular, rules. Do not continue to get tangled in thoughts and ideas of a layman. Those who strictly follow

the monastic rules will find their minds at ease and unfettered.

98 Unlike things in this world, everything in the Pure Land has neither color nor form. Do not project the ways in which we live in this world, such as what we eat, wear, etc., to the Pure Land because such projection reflects our sense of greed as well as our attachment to the form. If you are attached to the form, your cravings will create disturbances in your mind while meditating. This can be quite dangerous, especially when you lack the ability to control and stabilize your own mind. Therefore, do not cling to the images derived from "color and form," for the world "without color and form" is beyond our imagination.

99 We all have accumulated immeasurable and illimitable negative karma over the eons. These entanglements are the cause of the tremendous obstacles we encounter during our practice. Therefore, we must repent every day; further, we should vow to break out of the cycle of birth and death and to deliver all sentient beings. Only through such practice can we attain ultimate enlightenment.

100 The path of practice can never be free of obstacles. Where there are people, there are disputes, annoyances, conflicts and all sorts of disagreeable cir-

cumstances. Rather than expecting a smooth path, you ought to strengthen your willpower when confronting difficulties. Remember, when your attention does not focus on adversities, you will neither cling to them nor be vexed by them. Then, you will be able to practice with an unfettered mind.

101 The greatest blessing of human rebirth is the ability to practice; indeed, we ought to seize this opportunity and practice the best we can. However, do not cling to any specific asceticism, such as no food or no sleep, for this will be practice with an attachment to the "form." Not only will it spoil your health, but it also will leave your mind scattered and restless. If you haven't attained a certain level, how can you possibly benefit from that kind of asceticism? Therefore, practice should be guided by right mindfulness; the true path lays in the wisdom of ordinariness.

102 Practice should begin with training your "mind" to the extent that it's pure and clean. If, on the other hand, you keep your eyes mainly on others, finding their faults and making comments, you will only create animosities among people and breed vexations for yourself; you will not be able to cultivate your mind, nor will it become pure. Therefore, practicing purification of the mind means observ-

ing yourself carefully, being watchful of the incipience of each and every thought of yours.

103 The *Heart Sutra* states: "Perceive that the five
skandhas are empty thereby transcending all
sufferings." This means that, in order to transcend
all sufferings, we must eliminate our adherence to
the four forms of existence: self, others, sentient
beings, and life, as well as our attachment to the
myriad colors and forms of this world.
Unfortunately, most of us are not able to forgo our
physical desires and continue to be swayed by the
form, sound, smell, taste, touch, and other qualities of material appearances. And it is precisely
due to this inability to forgo our clinging to
worldly affinities that we cannot be relieved from
our suffering.

104 Sakyamuni Buddha used to practice "bodily sacrifice" to attain buddhahood and deliver sentient
beings. But he did it all spontaneously, not a bit
forced. You see, when a practitioner attains a state
of *samadhi* and no longer clings to a set form of
existence (either self, others, sentient beings, or
life), he naturally feels no pain. But most of us
have yet to attain that level and are bound to the
form of "self;" we are pained even when pricked by
a pin or stung by a mosquito. Because we have yet
to reach that state of *samadhi* our minds and

senses will spontaneously react to external agitation, and we are easily susceptible to painful feelings. Therefore, we must not practice compulsory
bodily sacrifice; otherwise, it will become a form
of attachment.

105 Asceticism does not mean that we should force
ourselves to do what are beyond our capabilities.
Rather, it is about the resolve to accomplish tasks
that are difficult and challenging, to tolerate what
may seem intolerable, to eat what others would not
eat, and to do what others would not do.

106 To believe, to resolve, and to practice--"practice"
should follow a vow to perform the discipline of
the faith; without it there would be no practice.
Take Bodhisattva Ksitigarbha for example. He
vowed not to attain buddhahood until all hell-
beings are delivered. Because the Bodhisattva has
tremendous compassion for all beings, this grand
vow he made bestowed on him the buddha quality.
Hence, those who tread the bodhisattva-path
continue to strive for the benefit of others. The
essence of such practice is "selflessness." Even
though this path emphasizes delivering others
while striving for self-salvation, you yourself
would have been liberated before all beings are
delivered.

107 It may come to pass that we pledge to do certain
things but lack a strong enough willpower to carry
it through, often giving up when things get rough.
This, then, is not a genuine vow. There are grand
vows and minor ones. What we should make are
grand vows, i.e. vows that are without set "form or
color." Therefore, put your mind into carrying out
your vows, not just announcing them! Whatever
challenges you encounter or circumstances you
come across, strive to maintain the tranquility of
your mind while making no distinction between
likes and dislikes. Continuation of such practice
will gradually reduce your vexations while freeing
your mind and body. So, practice by adhering to
your own vows! Vows are the seeds of our practice
that will eventually bear fruits. Without firm vows,
nothing can be accomplished.

108 Amitabha Buddha made forty-eight grand vows to
deliver sentient beings while Bodhisattva
Ksitigarbha vowed not to attain buddhahood until
the hells are empty. However, despite all the grand
vows buddhas and bodhisattvas made to assist us
breaking free of the cycle of birth and death, all
beings remained unenlightened, roaming among
the six divisions of rebirth. We keep on our pursuit of sensual satisfaction, clinging to our greed,
anger, and ignorance as well as other pains such as
parting from the beloved. As we mistake all these

illusions for reality, we can not be enlightened. That is why the compassionate Amitabha Buddha made his forty-right grand vows to deliver all beings, hoping that we will be able to transcend the six divisions of rebirth, shake off our misery, and attain eternal happiness. Now, if our vows correspond with these forty-eight vows, Amitabha Buddha will guide us along the way; and when we die, we will be reborn in the Pure Land.

109 Most people are active and their minds tend to be restless. However, a practitioner must constantly maintain the tranquility of the mind, i.e., the mind ought to be serene at all times regardless of circumstances. If you can sit quietly without sensing too much, or be vexed by, external turmoil, just feeling tranquil and at ease, then you are on the right track.

110 As we know, all beings in this world have cravings, which in turn generate illimitable and immeasurable vexations. Most of our cravings are for physical gratification and can only be restrained if we remain contented. There is an old saying: "Contentment leads to ceaseless joy." This may sound simple, but is by no means easy to carry out. Yet, it is undeniable that whenever you feel contented, your mind will be free of vexations and attachments and will stay pure and unfettered.

111 If we monastic practitioners were contented, we would carve for nothing and be free of all vexa- tions derived from attachments. Unfortunately, our minds remain easily distracted by external envi- ronments, and all sorts of unruly ideas instanta- neously come forth as we see, hear, and eat. Even though you make no explicit demand, but the fact that you have these ideas betrays your craving. Therefore, contentment means "craving for noth- ing," a principle crucial to our practice. If we stay contented at all times, our minds will not be swayed by ever-changing circumstances.

112 We practitioners ought to relinquish our attach- ments all the time so that we would be free of secular concerns towards the end of our lives. If you continue to indulge yourself, there is the grave danger that you may go astray at this crucial moment of rebirth. Therefore, try to maintain the serenity of your mind while discarding all distinc- tions between good and bad. You will then attain the state of "mindlessness." This, however, does not mean that you have become indifferent; rather, it means that you have let go of your sense of dis- crimination. The attainment of such a state will then be a clear indication of your genuine prowess in practice.

113 Cravings for "wealth, lust, fame, food, and sleep" will lead us straight to hell! Not knowing it, we are all entangled in these five cravings, unable to break out of the relentless cycle of birth and death. Therefore, the reason for our leaving home for practice is to purify our minds so that we can be free from the constraints of our own sensual passions.

114 In order to become monastic practitioners, we all have "renounced" the secular way of life. Now, the word "renounce" is crucial. What exactly do we need to renounce? We have to renounce our physical desires and sentimental attachments. Not only should we let go of our cravings for good clothing, tasty food, lavish housing, etc., but also of our emotional attachments to our beloved parents, spouses, and children. All our attachments should go. Really let go!

115 While you practice, be sure to let go of both your mind and your body. Otherwise, your dignified meditation posture only belies a mind overflowed with illusive and erroneous ideas. Under the circumstances, you will have great difficulty retaining right mindfulness. If your mind is preoccupied with misleading thoughts, the illusive mind is in charge. On the other hand, if your mind thinks of nothing but "buddha," then buddha is your mind.

You should let go of the body, the mind, and the world; just concentrate on reciting the Buddha's name so as to foster right mindfulness. In order to retain right mindfulness when we are dying, we have to practice this all the time. This is crucial because it will determine whether we can attain buddhahood or continue to roam in the cycle of birth and death.

116 One of the goals of practice is to eliminate the sense of greed. When tainted by the evil seeds of greed, our minds will easily become scattered and we will not be able to retain right mindfulness. Thereupon, our minds will be swamped with evil ideas and become restless and discontented, which in turn will create endless delusive vexations. Under the circumstances, we can never feel free nor at ease.

117 Vegetarian diet is a positive auxiliary cause for practice, and also a good method to keep the precept against killing. Be aware that the karmic obstructions created by killing for food eventually have to be repaid in full; there is no escape from the laws of causality and rebirth. Eliminating our desire for food, the satisfaction of which cost the lives of other beings, brings a great relief. Not only will we be free of enslaving ourselves just to satisfy the desire of our mouth, but we also will avoid

creating more negative karma while cultivating
our sentiments of lovingkindness and compassion.
Therefore, vegetarian diet will help to purify and
liberate our minds; it is also a method to practice
relinquishing the attachments of our sense organs
to the six *gunas* (sense objects).

118 The five *kasaya* periods of impurity contain all the
negative habitual patterns, vexations, and sinister
seeds all beings accumulated through the eons.
Derived from contact of the sense organs with the
six *gunas,* these negative elements are enacted by
our sense of discernment, which lead to distinction
and discrimination. These distinctions will bring
forth the fruits of the sinister seeds and accumulated karmic obstructions, which in turn create the
five *kasaya* periods of impurity (i.e. periods of
increasing calamities, erroneous views, vexations,
miseries, and shortening of human life).

119 Our practice should aim at attaining both merit
and wisdom. "Take refuge in the Buddha and
attain twofold satisfaction." The two folds are merit
and wisdom. Where does merit come from? It
grows out of forbearance. With genuine forbearance, we can accumulate merits and eventually
will be able to enjoy blessed rewards and reduce
our negative karma. When all our karmic obstructions are eradicated, our buddha-wisdom will

unfold. Thus, "forbearance" is the first principle of the path to buddhahood. Those who practice forbearance will attain supreme enlightenment.

120 One basic principle of monastic practice is to eliminate our sense of greed. We can start by eliminating our cravings for the six *gunas* (sense objects); this is the initial step to break out of the cycle of birth and death. As we know, greed derived from the contact of the six sense organs with the six *gunas* and enacted by our sense of discernment, which leads to distinction and discrimination. We have to expel greed from where it originates. Such practice is fundamental and is crucial to whether we can escape samsara or not.

121 Things do not happen to us by accident. Rather, they all have their roots in the karmic affinities we created in the past. If we fostered good affinities in previous lives, we will enjoy this life; otherwise, we will be dissatisfied, even troubled or pained. A practitioner should understand that things arise according to conditions and have no inherent existences of their own. When we feel distressed or dissatisfied, we should know that the ways things are are merely the results of certain conditions, not reality in itself. Hence, there is no need to cling to disconcerting sentiments, or be perturbed by them. Such a change of perception according to Buddhadharma will free us from the grip of pain.

122 The fact that in this life we attain human existence and take refuge in the Three Jewels (Buddha, Dharma, and *Sangha*) is due to our practice in previous lives. We might have prostrated, made offerings and almsgiving in the temple, or recited the name of the Buddha, etc. thus planted seeds of good affinity with the Buddha. But why take refuge? Sakyamuni Buddha taught us that there are eight kinds of misery from which we constantly suffer: birth, aging, disease, death, separation from loved ones, company of hated ones, failure to obtain what we desire, and all the ills of the five *skandhas*. As long as we remain in human forms, there can be no escape from such pains. The only way out of this bitter sea of rebirths is to take refuge in the Three Jewels and practice according to the teachings of the Buddha.

123 The law of causality applies to everyone, whether you are a lay person or a monastic practitioner; it also applies to everything that happens in this universe. For instance, the reason that we are able to leave home for practice is due to the good seeds we planted in our previous lives. Our monastic practice, on the other hand, will pave the way for our attaining buddhahood in the future. Hence, where there is a cause, there is a result; everything we do, even just an idea that crosses the mind, will have its effect. All teachings of the Buddha

recorded in the sutras are premised on this law of "cause and effect." Good cause brings good result. Accordingly, we must have "right" reasons to become monastic practitioners, i.e. a vow to attain supreme enlightenment for the deliverance of all sentient beings, and a desire to be relieved from the circle of birth and death. If you entered a monastery because you experienced unbearable blows or because you wished to evade hardships or reality, you would not have the firm determination indispensable for monastic practice. You might easily be overtaken by evil ideas and would not be able to retain right mindfulness. We all need a strong resolve when entering the monastery so that we can overcome all adversities--however difficult they may be. No attainment of buddhahood is possible without it. Therefore, the Buddha taught us to repent and make grand vows so that we can tread the path of practice with success.

124 In the eons, we all have accumulated immeasur-able and illimitable karmic obstructions through killing. For example, immeasurable beings con-tained in the rice are killed so that we may have a bowl of rice. Further, using pesticide in growing farm products is also a form of killing. Despite the fact that we do not commit these killings directly, we still have to bear certain consequences. If we fail to practice diligently to ensure our rebirth in

the Pure Land, we can not even redeem the karma resulting from such indirect killings in this life!

125 We monastic practitioners ought to have strong resolve. Do not be perturbed by petty agitation or minor diseases. Rather, we should count our blessings that we sowed the seeds in previous lives thus have attained the opportunity to leave home for practice. If, however, our resolve wavers due to ill health, it indicates a lack of wisdom on our part and the fact that we are reigned by our physical body. Hence, show your determination! A vow to attain total enlightenment will enable us to overcome all adversities and eradicate all vexations. Every cause has its effect, as every effect arises from a cause. Do not sow more seeds of rebirth into this world; sow seeds of liberation from the cycle of birth and death. If we constantly recite the name of Amitabha Buddha and keep our minds pure and free of vexations, we are sowing good seeds that will result in our attainment of buddhahood and our rebirth in the Pure Land. Once we have sowed the seeds of reciting the name of the Buddha, it is certain that we will reap the fruits of attaining buddhahood.

126 Monastic practitioners should vow to work for the benefit of others so as to accumulate felicities and merits. We should be willing to do whatever others

refuse to do, and pay attention to things others ignore. Pick up unfinished chores when others are taking a break; do not complain that "such is not my assignment thus not my business." Otherwise, not only would we accumulate no merit, but we also can not expect any breakthrough in our practice. So, constantly offer yourself to serve public interests. You should know that, even though monastic practice is the supreme dogma, without consistently dwelling on it, you would not attain buddhahood.

127 The purpose of attending an intensive seven-day retreat on reciting the name of the Buddha is to let us fully comprehend the doctrine of "no birth nor death," i.e. to see clearly the path of birth and death and to retrieve our intrinsic nature.

128 When attending an intensive seven-day retreat on reciting the Buddha's name, your mind should concentrate on the name of "Amitabha Buddha." Recite the name with full concentration; do not unleash your mind lest it should be distracted or swayed by external circumstances. Continue your recitation uninterrupted to the point that your mind is undivided and free of perplexity.

129 The purpose of attending an intensive seven-day retreat is to tame our bewildered minds so that we

can concentrate only on the name of the Buddha. Therefore, while in the retreat, we should train ourselves to be single-minded, i.e. whatever we do, we ought to have no thought other than the name of the Buddha, be it walking, staying, sitting, or sleeping.

130 In the eons, all beings continue to sow seeds in their eighth field of cognition; some of the seeds are good, but more significant are the immeasurable and illimitable evil ones. The purpose for our attending a seven-day retreat on reciting the name of the Buddha is to sow good seeds and to weed out the evil ones from our eighth field of cognition.

131 To deliver other beings is by no means an easy matter. With enough merit and karmic affinity to the Buddha accumulated in your previous lives as well as a certain degree of wisdom through diligent practice in this life, all bodhisattvas guarding the Dharma will come to assist you in your attempt to deliver others. Otherwise, no matter how hard you try, all the efforts will be in vain.

132 Our karmic obstructions are manifested in our vexations and in the numerous hindrances to our minds. For example, worrying about family members is a common form of impediment. We all

worry about different things, but largely ignore the most important one: how to escape the cycle of birth and death--we do not even care where we will be going after death.

133 If you have faith in the Buddha, practice according to the Dharma and repent past transgressions, you can then eradicate your karmic obstructions with the assistance of the Buddha. On the other hand, if you are not aware of this fact and fail to practice diligently, the strength of your negative karma will prevail and confine you to the eternal prison of rebirths.

134 If you still think of "how to sit, how to introspect" while practicing sitting meditation, you are not on the right track. This is an indication that you still cling to the sense of self and are attached to the "form," or outward appearances, of practice. The dual practice of Zen and Pure Land must begin with purifying the six sense organs. Keeping the precepts is the foundation for practicing Zen.

135 Practice should begin with asceticism, i.e. renouncing the body. Do not attend too much to the need of your body, which is nothing but an illusive shell case; do not put yourself in the fore-front of all your concerns, nor be calculating only of your own interests. Relinquish all attachments to your physical desires!

136　In this bitter sea of birth and death, all beings are struggling for survival--laboring for food, striving to transcend their misery. In the mountains, under the sea, and in the air, sentient beings search for food in their surroundings; they kill and eat the smaller and weaker species, though can not escape death in the end. They are thereby confined to the eternal prison of rebirths; without the will and diligent practice, they can never escape the bitter sea of samsara.

137　As a human being, no one can avoid the pain of birth, aging, disease, and death. Once we recognize this fact, we should try to escape from this misery. The most appropriate means that can guarantee us a genuine liberation from suffering is to practice Buddhadharma; it is also the only means that can deliver us from all trammels of life.

138　It is possible that some lay practitioners, while not comprehending fully the essence of Buddhism, may interpret incorrectly the teachings of the Buddha. We monastic practitioners ought to enlighten them when appropriate. Do not allow them to hold on to their misconceptions thus hinder their progress in practice. Otherwise, we are guilty of neglecting our responsibility.

139 It is not easy for the laity to practice without inter-
ruption. Consequently, it is difficult for them to
even liberate themselves, not to mention deliver
others. In practice, we should first try to restrain
our own scattered minds. Otherwise, with our
minds dispersed and easily distracted, how can we
expect to deliver others? The purpose of our being
born with the illusive existence of five *skandhas*
(i.e. our physical body) is to practice restraining
and liberating our scattered minds.

140 Some people may find themselves become even
more vexed after practice for a period of time. This
is due to the manifestation of their karmic
obstructions. Under these circumstances, they
ought to purify their deeds, words, and thoughts so
as to eradicate their deep-rooted karmic obstructions.

141 Where do all our ideas come from? They originate
from our delusion and from the imperfect senses
of our eyes, ears, nose, tongue, body, and mind.
Ideas arise when we see, hear, and try to make
distinctions of the messages received by our sense
organs.

142 You ought to understand that, while working for
the benefit of others, you are in fact working for
your own interests. Also, purification of the six

senses begins with purifying your own mind. If you crave even just a blade of grass, you will remain in the cycle of rebirths.

143 The best means to restrain our sensual organs from creating more negative karma is to recite the name of the Buddha. When recitation is done with an undivided mind, all voices will sound like recitation of the Buddha's name. Furthermore, we have to practice forbearance. After attaining a high-level of forbearance, we will be enlightened and can grasp the essence of everything we encounter.

144 Provide your mind is pure and clean, you can practice Zen in whatever you do, be it walking, staying, sitting, or sleeping. The initial step is to let go of all your worldly attachments; even the slightest attachment can impede your practice of Zen. These days, people keep asking me how to practice Zen. What they do not realize is that, because they are clinging tightly both to their families and to their pursuits of fame and wealth, it is very difficult for them to practice Zen. This is also true for monastic practitioners. If monks or nuns still run after fame and wealth, or desire lavish food and housing, how can they expect to attain *samadhi* (perfect absorption) when practicing meditation? To say that they are practitioners of Zen is deceiving.

145 Monastic practitioners deliver others by teaching the Dharma; lay people can practice offering with all sincerity and be respectful to the Buddha, the Dharma, and the *Sangha*.

146 No one can attain enlightenment just by seeking instruction of Buddhadharma from a Master. All sutras are maps that mark the paths practitioners may take. Only through diligent practice, not pronouncements, will we be able to comprehend the teachings of the Buddha and attain various stages.

147 We can "learn" secular knowledge, but we can never pretend that we are able to "learn" Buddhadharma in a similar fashion as we do secular knowledge. Hampered by our imperfect perception, as all ordinary people are, we can never truly comprehend the essence of the sutras through research or study. Thus, you may very well think that you understand the meaning of a sutra after reading it. But your understanding is as illusive as the flower's reflection in the mirror or the moon's reflection on the water because it is derived more from your imagination and speculation than from a genuine comprehension attested through practice. Therefore, you should not cling to the words of any sutra and adopt a literal interpretation of what you read. Otherwise, you will be

bound by the words and can not attain true liberation. In the *Diamond Sutra*, the Buddha taught us:
"one should relinquish even the Dharma; how
much more so undharmic doctrines." All sutras are
paths pointed out by the Buddha to help us escape
the cycle of birth and death. The purpose of study-
ing them is to follow the paths, to practice diligently so as to attest the teachings. There is no
other way to escape the cycle of birth and death
but to practice in person. Have faith that all
buddhas are guiding and watching over us so that
we can ultimately reach nirvana and unfold the
formless wisdom immanent in the essence of our
minds.

.2.

On Keeping the Precepts

1   The purpose of (receiving) the precepts is to remind us to be alert of our own thoughts and conduct. When we repent over any and every transgression, we are keeping the precepts.

2   When I say keeping the precepts, I do not mean that we should cling to the "form" of precepts, i.e. adhere to the precepts word for word. If you take such a literal approach, not only will you put yourself in a straitjacket, but you will also be at odds with the rest of the world. You will become judgmental and are prone to find fault with others thereby increase your own vexations. Therefore, the key is to observe the quintessence of the precepts, i.e., purify your deeds, words, and thoughts through keeping them. Basically, you should "be kind and compassionate to all beings while providing them with expedient guidance for practice." Whatever you do, observing this principle will safeguard you against possible breach of the precepts.

3   To a large extent, receiving the precepts means practicing forbearance. If you can be free of agitation, vexation, and violent reaction while listening to an insult or accusation against you, you are keeping the precepts.

4   The purpose of receiving the precepts is to safeguard our own minds, not to be critical to others. After we receive the precepts, their formless embodiment dwelling in our eighth field of cognition will come forth to prevent us from breaching them. Therefore, we should use the precepts as our mentor and solemnly keep them so that our minds can be in accord with *prajna* (wisdom).

5   The purpose of receiving the precepts is to guard our own behavior, rather than using the criteria to find fault with others. Otherwise, we will be creating negative karma through our words, which is a breach of the precepts in itself.

6   Receiving the precepts is the beginning of our practice. We should use the precepts as our mentor and practice accordingly.

7   If your sense organs are impure, your false or misleading thoughts continue, and your ignorance remains, then you can not be enlightened. When

the Master hits you with the incense board in the meditation hall, he is hitting your ignorance and delusion. Therefore, you should restrain your sense organs and purify your deeds, words, and thoughts. Keep the precepts to the extent that the six sense objects can no longer contaminate your sense organs. This is the first step and the foundation of the practice of Zen.

8   There ought to be a difference after receiving the precepts. Afterwards, you should be more keen to ascetic practice, more eager to get rid of bad habits and evil thoughts, and should learn a great deal from the precepts.

9   Be patient and tolerant while receiving the precepts, then you are entering into the path of practice. Daily life ought to be simple--do not make a fuss. Do not complain about trivial things such as the bed is not cozy, or the food taste awful, etc. The purpose of holding a session to receive the precepts is to learn proper conduct and manners, not to build up connections, or to gossip about others thus create more karma of words.

10   What do we mean by keeping the precepts? It means watching closely the incipience of each and every one of our thoughts and ideas. All precepts

are designed to tame our minds and to eradicate our vexations. The precepts represent the Buddha's conduct and *samadhi*, the state of the Buddha's mind. If a practitioner faithfully keeps the precepts without going astray in all deeds, words, and thoughts, his mind will be completely purified. He can then attain right *samadhi* and his immanent buddha-wisdom will unfold. Therefore, "the precepts are the foundation of *bodhi* (enlightenment)." Only by keeping the precepts can we attain *samadhi*, wisdom will naturally follow. Hence, "*sila* (precepts), *samadhi* (perfect absorption), and *prajna* (wisdom)" are inseparable. Only with the restraint of the precepts can we avoid transgressions that would confine us in samsara. Therefore, our mind-set is most crucial in keeping the precepts.

11 Among the five basic precepts, the most commonly violated ones are killing and lying. And we should pay special attention to the precept against lying, either as a slander, false boasting, or deception. What we say can help as well as destroy others. Kind words please people, vicious ones hurt; but most words exchanged are gossip that can only create karma of words. Quarrelling or debating with others will also make our minds scattered and restless. That is why "bodhisattvas are fearful of causes, sentient beings, retributions." We practi-

tioners should also pay particular attention to comprehend this emphasis on "causes." Bodhisattvas can perceive the cause and effect of each and every move hence will never take any action that can lead to harsh retribution. But most people regret only after they have tasted the bitter fruits of their misconduct. That is why it is always too late when they sigh: "had I known the consequences, I would never have done such and such things!" Therefore, the basic principal Sakyamuni Buddha expounded for our guidance in the precepts and sutras is the law of causality. Only by closely observe this principal will the results of our deeds be satisfactory.

12 Laymen often indulge themselves in the pursuit of fame and wealth thereby remaining in the cycle of rebirths. Monastic practitioners, on the other hand, diligently keep the precepts, meditate, and develop their wisdom in the hope of escaping the cycle of birth and death.

13 You should practice harder after receiving the precepts. Solemnly keep the precepts and endure all hardships so as to attain *samadhi,* and *prajna*. When you reach this stage, your words can naturally deliver other people, even the ghosts and spirits that come to hear you can be freed of their miseries. This is what we called "delivering others

while working on your own liberation." At that stage, guardians of the Dharma will also come to assist you.

14 We monastic practitioners should use the precepts as our mentor and practice diligently to the extent that, when meeting us, people will feel the bliss of meeting a buddha and will naturally respect and admire us.

.3.

On Reciting the Name of the Buddha

1   We all know that everyone suffers from vexations, though not necessary know that, as long as vexations last, we will remain in the cycle of birth and death. Therefore, we ought to seize the opportunity of this short human rebirth to concentrate on reciting the name of the Buddha and practice diligently to eradicate all vexations. Otherwise, we will remain in samsara and perpetually wander among the six divisions of rebirth.

2   Whatever circumstances you encounter, always remember to recite "Amitabha Buddha;" whenever you wish to steer clear of conflict, recite the name as well. In short, recite the Buddha's name whenever you have a moment to yourself, even if you should fall asleep amidst recitation. This practice will help you transcend the three realms of existence (the realms of sensual desire, of form and formless ness) and be reborn in the Pure Land. Therefore, when disturbances arise during practice, pretend not to see or hear them. Do not be

distracted by the six sense objects, nor be swayed by circumstances. Just continue reciting "Amitabha Buddha."

3 Reciting the name of the Buddha with an undivided mind will lead to the realization of the essence of your own mind.

4 Many who do not understand the significance of reciting the name of the Buddha suppose the only attainment possible through this practice is a long life. However, if instead of practicing to escape samsara, you only create more negative karma by killing and other misconduct, what is the use of a long life? You still remain in the cycle of rebirths, wandering among the six divisions of sentient existence! The matter of escaping the cycle of birth and death is so crucial, yet life is so impermanent. If you truly comprehend the rationale of why we should escape the cycle of birth and death, you will, without hesitation, seize the opportunity of this human rebirth to practice reciting the name of Amitabha Buddha so that you can be reborn in the Pure Land.

5 Reciting the name of Amitabha Buddha is truly a pure and proper path, a path that will lead to the Pure Land. When we recite "Amitabha Buddha" in unison, all with an undivided mind, we can arrive

at the Pure Land. There is no need to purchase tickets, as the dharmic vehicle to the Pure Land is formless and colorless.

6   Life is so impermanent; it can easily end in a breath. Therefore, we should seize every moment to practice diligently. Don't waste more time; keep on reciting the name of the Buddha. This is the most important thing for us here and now!

7   Keep on reciting the name of the Buddha, whether we are moving, staying, sitting, or sleeping! If we observe closely, we will find that most of the time, instead of concentrating on the name of Amitabha Buddha, our minds are easily distracted by external environments and wandering all over the places. If we can not restrain our minds and allow them to be swayed by circumstances, there is no way we can ever escape samsara.

8   You can practice Zen in all your daily activities, be it walking, staying, sitting, or sleeping, not just in "sitting" meditation. If you constantly maintain the serenity and impartiality of your mind, you are practicing Zen. To be more specific, Zen means an undivided mind.

9   It is by no means easy to practice reciting the name of the Buddha. You have to relinquish all worldly

concerns and recite with a pure and undivided mind so as to be in accord with the Buddha. Recite "Namah Amitabha Buddha" clearly and listen attentively without any doubt, all your scattered thoughts will naturally be expelled. You can then practice with an undivided mind free of perplex-ity.

10 If you have faith in my teaching, remember to recite the Buddha's name constantly whether you are walking, staying, sitting, or sleeping. Hold on to it even in your dreams. You can thereby be free of greed and worldly desires and your mind will not be perturbed. When you reach this stage, the Pure Land will naturally come forth before you. Do not take this matter lightly! It pertains to whether you can escape the cycle of birth and death.

11 The *Larva of Chilo simplex* (a kind of moth) can not have offspring. They pick other bugs, put them in the soil, and speak to them incessantly: "Be like me! Be like me!" When the bugs come out of the soil, they grow to be like *Chilo simplex.* We should follow this example in our practice: shun from myriad temptations, just recite "Amitabha Buddha, Amitabha Buddha" with an undivided mind. After continuous practice, the recitation will become your second nature and you will ultimately attain buddhahood.

12   When you are at home, practice prostration and recite the Buddha's name whenever possible. Don't waste your time gossiping or chattering! Then you can hope to be liberated from samsara and be reborn in the Pure Land.

13   Do not be perturbed by erroneous and illusive thoughts; just ignore them when they emerge. If you keep on reciting "Amitabha Buddha," such thoughts will gradually diminish.

14   Try to comprehend and experience the essence of the Dharma through each and every move you take so that evil ideas will have no chance to come forth. Otherwise, your life will be wasted. When not guided by right mindfulness, you may be overwhelmed by illusive and erroneous thoughts even though not pronouncing them, and remain clinging to, hence being vexed by, your biased judgments of worldly affairs. Continue living like this and you will have no chance of escaping samsara. The most important thing in your life, therefore, is to foster right mindfulness and practices the supreme Dharma that would set you free of all the trammels of life.

15   Smile when things are going well, the same when times are bad, for "good" or "bad" are nothing but arbitrary distinctions made by the mind, no need

to differentiate or discriminate. When feeling happy, keep pondering "who is the one that is happy?" and when vexed, asking "who is the one that is full of defilement?" You should know that vexations and illusive ideas are also part of your mind, your "perturbed" mind. Pay no attention, though, when they emerge, just keep on reciting "Amitabha Buddha" clearly and distinctly. Continue this practice long enough, the illusive thoughts will naturally diminish. The instant the mind becomes pure and undivided, it is the buddha-mind.

16 Don't think too much; just work, eat, and recite the name of the Buddha! Live only for today and let tomorrow be tomorrow. Let go of all worries and anxieties. Such is an indication of firm resolution, and such is practice.

17 "The nature of Dharma is emptiness. It has no place of origin nor destination." Thus, when you are vexed or angry, do not insist on locating the source of your vexation or anger. If you do, you will neither be happy nor be able to concentrate on practice, let alone making any progress! You have to relinquish all concerns and let go of all fetters. The most important thing is to keep "Amitabha Buddha" in your mind!

18 Reciting the name of the Buddha requires uninter-
    rupted long-term practice, like the water of small
    streams keep running into the sea. No matter how
    many times you recite per day, you have to do it
    every day and with an undivided mind. This is the
    only way for your recitation to stream into the sea
    of the great vows of Amitabha Buddha (i.e. be in
    accord with the vows) and you can thereby hope
    to be reborn in the Pure Land. Consequently, any-
    one who is willing to recite the name of the
    Buddha is half way toward attaining buddhahood.

19 It is by no means easy to practice reciting the name
    of the Buddha because the recitation has to be
    done with an undivided mind and each word
    pronounced distinctly. Without the guidance of
    right mindfulness, your mind may become scat-
    tered and all sorts of unruly ideas may spring up.
    Under such circumstances, your recitation can
    easily become a mindless utterance that can never
    be in accord with the great vows of Amitabha
    Buddha. Indeed, recitation with an undivided mind
    requires a strong resolve. Otherwise, how can
    anyone expect to practice well when his/her mind
    is overwhelmed by illusive and erroneous
    thoughts?

20 There will be immense disturbances and obstacles
    to our minds while practicing recitation, mostly

caused by incessant illusive thoughts. Since our minds are basically unstable and can easily be swayed by our thoughts, it is difficult to recite the name of the Buddha, even just once, with an undivided mind.

21 We all have accumulated immeasurable bad seeds in the eons. Without diligent practice, we will only increase our karmic obstructions and live this life in vain. Once losing human rebirth, we might not be able to regain such a good opportunity for practice for eons. In that case, when can we hope to escape the cycle of birth and death? Knowing the consequences, it will be wise for us to forgo all worldly attachments at once and practice diligently. Only when we realize that our physical body is nothing but a temporary and illusive shell case, and that we all have a buddha-nature that can neither be born nor be extinguished, will we be able to attain eternal liberation.

22 All of us are born with negative karma accumulated in past lives; that is why we remain in this cycle of rebirths. So, if those who have poor health realize that their illnesses are largely due to their karmic obstructions, they should avoid killing and recite the Buddha's name more often. Such practice will gradually eradicate their karmic obstructions.

23 If you find yourself overwhelmed by incessant erroneous and illusive thoughts, you should keep yourself busy so that your ideas will have an anchor. Otherwise, with thoughts running wild, you can not practice reciting the name of the Buddha. But if you practice recitation while working, you will gradually forget that you are working hard. Besides, when you concentrate both on your tasks and on recitation, you will stop making distinctions about your environment, and your mind will naturally be free of discrimination.

24 For your daily practice, you should recite the name of the Buddha, dutifully carry out your monastic tasks, and constantly think of working for the benefit of others. This is the dual practice toward gaining merit and wisdom that will lead directly to liberation from the cycle of birth and death. On the other hand, if you only think of your own interests and never about others, you are neither kind nor compassionate; your practice won't go very far and you are sure to remain in samsara.

25 Practice reciting the name of the Buddha requires the trinity of faith, will, and action. Follow the recitation closely--whether pronouncing it or reciting in silence--you should be able to hear every word distinctly. If you practice to the extent that you hear nothing but the name of the Buddha,

that you neither distinguish nor be distracted by any other sound, you would have attained the stage of "an undivided mind free of perplexity."

26 Our tendency to have erroneous and illusive thoughts is rooted deeply. That is why we tend to feel dizzy or are easily distracted by illusive thoughts when we recite the name of the Buddha. Therefore, we have to keep reminding ourselves to restrain our minds while practicing recitation.

27 Some people take recitation lightly, thinking it easy to practice. But if you ask them to try it, they might soon be vexed after starting to recite the name of the Buddha, or they might feel oppressed by tons of rocks upon hearing the sound of recitation. Such negative reactions indicate that they did not plant good seeds in their previous lives and that their karmic obstructions are so enormous that they are unable to benefit from recitation. Therefore, do not look down upon the discipline of reciting the name of the Buddha.

28 Nowadays, many people claim to be Buddhists but in fact do not have right mindfulness. They make offerings to supernatural local deities praying for blessings and take it to be the practice of Buddhism. Or, they prostrate themselves in front of buddha statues because they want something in

return. They are chasing after wealth and fame, and are deluded by such illusive pursuits day in and day out. Without the guidance of right views, it will not be easy for such people to escape the cycle of birth and death.

29 We should make vows as grand as that of Bodhisattva Ksitigarbha, i.e. not to attain buddhahood until all beings are delivered. While treading the bodhisattva-path, this grand vow is a vow to attain buddhahood. If, on the other hand, we think only of ourselves, then we are neither kind nor compassionate; our practice will not go very far and our attachment to the form of "self" will remain. Clinging to the sense of self will only plant evil seeds such as vexation, attachment, discrimination, jealousy, greed, anger, and ignorance, etc., that will keep us in the cycle of birth and death. Hence, practice should always be motivated by altruism. And while working for the benefit of others, we will also benefit ourselves. Help others whenever and wherever possible and lead their minds to dwell on the Dharma. Whatever we do, if we are kind and compassionate to all beings while providing them with expedient guidance for practice, we are treading the bodhisattva-path.

30 Why are we besieged in the endless cycle of
rebirths? It is because we are heavily defiled and
attached to sensual attractions, and are vexed by
incessant cravings for wealth, sex, fame, food, and
sleep. Our unremitting pursuit of physical satisfaction, therefore, creates immeasurable negative
karma, which keeps us forever in samsara.

31 Whatever circumstances we run into, our first
thought should always be "reciting the name of the
Buddha," nothing else. We will then plant only
seeds of recitation in our eighth field of cognition.
Therefore, what we should practice daily is to
convert all sounds we hear, be it birds singing,
vehicles moving, or people talking, into sounds of
chanting Buddha, Dharma, and *Sangha*. That is to
say, instead of being distracted, we should inte-
grate all external noises and phenomena into our
practice of reciting the name of the Buddha.

32 "Becoming an impeccable person equals attaining
buddhahood." The Dharma is in itself complete,
adroit, and expedient. A practitioner should be
strict in disciplining him/herself but considerate
when dealing with others. Be patient in whatever
you do, be kind, compassionate, and tolerant to
whomever you meet, and help others when circumstances arise. By so doing, you are fostering
good affinity with all beings.

33 The essence of "seeking guidance" is to make use of all circumstances to examine our own minds, to see whether they are vexed, deluded, or discriminating. That is, we should observe the incipience of our each and every thought to ensure that our minds remain undiscriminating, undefiled, and unfettered. This is the true meaning of seeking guidance.

34 The most important thing for a practitioner is to recite the name of the Buddha with an undivided mind. The second is to practice "forbearance." Shut your ears and eyes, pretend not to see or hear when people say or do disagreeable things; instead, be gentle with them and do not become vexed. "Forbearance" is crucial in practice.

35 Practice reciting the name of the Buddha to the extent that "flowers flourish and the Buddha comes into view." We all have a buddha immanent in our minds. When we practice recitation to the extent that our minds are pure and free of vexations, we will meet the buddha within ourselves. Therefore, only by the extinction of all vexations can we attain the stage where "flowers flourish and the Buddha comes into view." We should practice compassion and forbearance in our daily lives while avoiding impulsiveness and petulance and controlling our temper. Be adroit and harmonious

when dealing with people and handle everything with the help of reason. Seek not the faults of others and do not be vexed by the rights or wrongs we perceive. Be gentle and kind to others, though not for the sake of building up connections. Treat everyone, be he/she moral or immoral, with equality and impartiality. Do not turn others away with an icy face. With every move intended for the benefit of others and done with sympathetic compassion, not only will we foster good affinity with others but our minds will be purified and ourselves free of all vexations. We are thereby attaining the stage where "flowers flourish and the Buddha comes into view."

36 Unless all emotional attachments are relinquished, merely reciting the Buddha's name with your tongue will not help you escape the cycle of birth and death. Recite with all sincerity and an undivided mind and relinquish myriad attachments, then you will be reborn in the Pure Land.

37 "The truth will come forth when you have faith; your prayers will be answered if you pray with sincerity." Recite the Buddha's name with all sincerity, then you will feel the auspiciousness indicating the presence of the Buddha. Have a deep conviction that buddhas and bodhisattvas fill the void of the universe. However, they only correspond with minds of utmost sincerity.

38 Reciting the name of the Buddha is very powerful in that it helps to eradicate our karmic obstructions and unfold our wisdom. But do not cling to the "form" of recitation; nor should you be attached to the color and form (i.e. physical existence) of this world. Otherwise, your mind can not be pure or liberated, i.e. you will remain in the confinement of the five *skandhas* (form, sensation, perception, volition, and consciousness), and your liberation will remain a daydream with no prospect of realization.

39 When practice recitation, you should do it with an undivided mind to the extent that "(your) mind is open and flowers (of your mind) flourish." That is to say when your mind is purified through recitation, you will naturally be free of vexations. When your mind is not crowded with destructive ideas generated by your greed, anger, and ignorance, it will not be inverted and, together with your body, will be free and at ease. When you attain that stage, this world is the Pure Land.

40 It takes a long time to attain any stage in practice. Therefore, we ought to practice training our minds all the time. For example, while others are chatting, practice recitation within our minds. Always be watchful lest our minds should become slack and scattered. Keep on reciting the Buddha's name; we can do it even while we are walking.

41 Right mindfulness is crucial for practicing recitation. Keep reciting "Namah Amitabha Buddha" and
you will naturally acquire right mindfulness.
Recitation should be done to the extent that your
mind never leaves the Buddha, nor the Buddha
your mind, and that your mind is undivided, free
of perplexity and inversion.

42 For lay practitioners, the best way to practice is to
recite the name of the Buddha. Also, better avoid
running around lest your mind should become
scattered and bewildered. Concentrate on your
recitation!

43 The purpose of reciting the name of the Buddha is
to restrain and stabilize our minds. We may not be
aware of it, but the reason we remain in the cycle
of rebirths is because our minds are always in a
state of fluctuation; they are swayed too easily by
ever-changing circumstances thereby confine us to
this eternal prison of birth and death. Therefore,
the purpose of recitation is to calm the mind.
Practice begins with the mind; liberation from
samsara also depends on the mind.

44 We all will run into numerous obstacles in the
course of practice. At times, we may feel overwhelmed by a problem and are consumed by the
ensuing delusion and vexations. But with a change

of perception, the seemingly formidable obstacle may be disposed of with ease. The purpose of practice, then, is to train our minds so that this "change of perception" will occur spontaneously. What we should keep in mind is the single notion of recitation. Constantly recite "Amitabha Buddha" in our minds. This will offset the seeds of delusion and vexations we have planted in our previous lives and help us transcend adversities through change of perceptions. When our minds are free of discrimination, feeling neither love nor distaste, we are in the state of *samadhi.*

45 Reciting the name of the Buddha helps us expel our erroneous and illusive thoughts. At the moment when not a single thought of ours is fraught with illusions and inversions, it is wisdom unfolding.

46 "Life is so impermanent that it can end within a breath." Instead of relying on others to recite the name of the Buddha at our deathbed, we should practice recitation all along to prepare ourselves for that crucial moment. Otherwise, there is little hope for us to be reborn in the Pure Land.

47 "Myriad Dharma originated from the mind." All circumstances are created by our minds. If our minds are unperturbed, everything will seem

stable, and we will have fewer worries. Recitation is a very powerful method. If we keep concentrating on reciting the Buddha's name, our minds will become unperturbed and unfettered. On the other hand, if our minds are under the full sway of our desires and circumstances, we will be confined to the cycle of rebirths forever. We should know that the merit of recitation is tremendous and that it is a great blessing for us to come across this discipline. By simply reciting "Amitabha Buddha," we can expect to escape the prison of birth and death and attain buddhahood.

48 How can our minds prevail over circumstances? One simple method is to keep reciting the name of the Buddha. Always keep in mind the name of "Amitabha Buddha!" This method suits most people. It is the easiest, fastest, and most direct way to practice, and is especially suitable for the contemporary people, whatever their capacity may be. Even an illiterate old lady can practice recitation well. The level you will attain depends solely on the strength of your faith. Never look down upon this simple phrase of "Namah Amitabha Buddha." Recitation is one of the methods of the Mahayana school and is by no means easy to practice. Master Yin-kuang once remarked that: "If one can recite 'Amitabha Buddha' well, it will be more than sufficient for one to attain buddhahood." Never

worry that you don't have enough time for practice. Whatever you do, if you keep reciting the
name of the Buddha, you are practicing.

49   There are many techniques for practicing recitation. Before attaining a certain level, we tend to
switch among various routines. Sometimes, we feel
one technique is particularly effective for restraining the mind. However, we may soon switch to
another routine because it seems more beneficial.
The "good" or "bad," though, are merely distinctions of our minds. Before attaining a certain level,
our minds are bound to be restless; it is a process
during the course of practice before our minds
finally settle for one routine. In fact, all techniques
are equally useful. Whether we give up one routine in favor of another, they are all choices made
by the essence of our minds. A diligent practitioner
will not cling to any specific routine. "It is the
essence of the mind that recites the name of the
Buddha and the same that listens." Recitation is
only an "idea" that flashes through our minds;
what's most important is that through recitation
we can make this flash of idea tranquil, stable, and
immovable.

50   When practice recitation, do not cling to the auspiciousness you experience, or dwell on any kind
of sensation, feeling, or form. Whatever you see or

feel, it is no more than a phantasm, a magical delusion. To dwell on such sensation or vision is quite dangerous! Do not brag about what you see during practice. All forms are nothing but your own illusions.

51 Buddha and *mara* (the tempter) exist only in our perception. Right mindfulness conceives buddha while evil thoughts generate *mara*. If you worry about family affairs and can't concentrate while reciting the Buddha's name, you have yet to attain right mindfulness. To practice means that you should relinquish all worldly concerns. If in the monastery your mind still lingers around your family, you are no different from a lay person, and this attachment is the source of your remaining in the cycle of birth and death. Concentrate on your practice and try to enlighten your family with Buddhadharma so that they can also be liberated. Otherwise, the entanglements between you and your family members will continue for endless lives to come and none of you can hope to escape samsara.

52 While practicing recitation, you may reach the state of samadhi where your mind is undivided and free of perplexity. Do not cling to such attainment. Feel no good or bad, love or distaste, indifference or attachment, success or failure, gain or

loss. Let all sentiments return to their original quiescent void, in which the brilliance of the essence of your mind will unfold.

53 If you wish to unfold your wisdom or to attain any specific stage through recitation, you are still clinging tightly to your sense of "self." All buddhas and bodhisattvas gain nothing and desire nothing.

54 The best way to counter erroneous and illusive thoughts springing up during your practice is simply to ignore them and continue your recitation. Worrying about "how to do away with the dispersed thoughts" will only add to your vexations. The more you recite the Buddha's name, the less likely it will be for illusive thoughts to arise. Besides, frequent recitation will also help to reduce your worldly desire and make it easier for your mind to become undivided.

.4.

On Reciting the Sutras

1   We Buddhists should make use of all available time
    to read and recite the sutras, perform prostration,
    recite the name of the Buddha, or practice sitting
    meditation. Do not let the time pass in vain and
    waste our lives.

2   The sutras are paths and antidotes we may take for
    our vexations. If you know how to apply the teach-
    ings in the sutras to help switching your percep-
    tion, vexations may be transformed into bodhi.
    This is the essence of sutra-recitation.
    Otherwise, vexations will only lead to delusion.

3   Instead of seeking liberation, sticking to your
    vexations is like taking the wrong medication
    when you are sick. It will entrench your ailment
    and make it even more difficult to cure. Prescribe
    the proper remedy to transform your vexations,
    then you would have found the direct path to the
    Pure Land.

4   Where can we find the sutras? They are in our
     minds. But this "heart sutra" immanent in every-
     one's mind can not be revealed without the unfold-
     ing of wisdom. All sutras expounded by Sakyamuni
     Buddha recorded buddha-wisdom; but since our
     own wisdom is yet to unfold, we tend to feel con-
     fused when reading the sutras. That is why we all
     have great difficulty either to comprehend the
     essence of "emptiness" or to immerse ourselves
     deeply in Buddhadharma.

5   All sutras are immanent within our minds, so are
     sila, samadhi, and *prajna* (precepts, perfect
     absorption, and wisdom). Verbal recitation of *sila,*
     samadhi, and *prajna* is of no use, though; you
     have to put them into practice, begin with disci-
     plining our body of the five *skandhas* (form, sen-
     sation, perception, volition, and consciousness).

6   When practice sutra-recitation, merely chanting
     with your tongue is not enough. You have to com-
     prehend the teachings and put them into practice
     to the extent that, without deliberation, your mind
     naturally is in accord with what you recite ver-
     bally. Otherwise, your practice will become just an
     exercise of the tongue. If you keep on clinging to
     the notion that "I am reciting the sutra" without
     comprehending what you are reciting, your mind
     will never correspond with the teachings of the
     sutra.

7   If you read the sutras and preach the Dharma
     without putting the teachings into practice, you
     are merely reciting others' ideas. It would be like
     counting treasures owned by others--however
     valuable they may be, they are not yours and won't
     help you escape the eternal prison of birth and
     death.

8   We should read the sermons, analects, and trea-
     tises of great Masters in the past as if they had not
     passed away and are still preaching and guiding
     us.

9   When people ask us to expound a certain sutra, we
     should do it sincerely and to the best of our abili-
     ties. It will benefit them as well as us. Do not be
     arrogant and pretend that you don't understand
     the sutra; otherwise, you will be at fault.

10   Try to comprehend the meaning of the sutra you
     are reading. Only through faith, comprehension,
     practice, and verification can the sutra help to
     unfold your immanent wisdom.

11   We ought to handle the sutras with great respect
     and utmost sincerity. In the old days, people used
     to pay a great deal of attention to such ideas as
     propriety, justice, honesty, and honor, and they
     also observed certain rules in their conduct, hence

the existence of saints. Nowadays, people tend to ignore such ideas and rules, hence the world in chaos.

.5.

On the Sense of Self

1   Most people are prone to criticize others and sing
     their own praises. Compliments bring them
     delight; criticism anger and distress. This is
     because they make a clear distinction between "self
     and others." If you enter practice without relin-
     quishing this kind of distinction, your mind can
     never be settled. Because when you cling to the
     sense of "self," you are bound to see everything
     only in "your own way," and value only your own
     ideas. The discriminative and calculating mind
     thus arose would in turn hamper your practice,
     increase your vexations, and keep you from eradi-
     cating your karmic obstructions.

2   Most people like to "listen" so as to gather infor-
     mation and find out whether anyone speaks ill of
     them. They also like to "discern" the mood of
     others and act upon it. All these are habitual pat-
     terns of common people, i.e. they are easily dis-
     tracted by events that do not concern them and
     they have a strong desire to please others for per-

sonal gains. This type of conduct will have an adverse effect on their practice.

3   Learn not to differentiate or discriminate so as to relinquish your attachment to the sense of "self," then wisdom will unfold. If you continue to cling to the sense of "self," you can not expect to attain any level in your practice.

4   All vexations in this world are caused by constant conflicts between self and others. We should see whether our practice could obliterate the distinction between self and others and also eliminate discrimination and calculation. The first step is to practice "forbearance," which is also the foundation of our practice. Do not insist that you are always right, for such assertion only indicates that you haven't acquired right mindfulness thereby act more like an ordinary person than a practitioner.

5   In order to eliminate attachments to the sense and form of self, you can begin by lessening your cravings for tasty food and lavish clothing. After a while, your sensual passions will be greatly reduced. You will then become less discriminating and will gradually enter the path of liberation that makes no distinctions among the forms of self, others, sentient beings, and life.

6   Don't always keep your eyes on the faults of others.
    Instead, reflect more on whether you yourself have
    made mistakes or are in the wrong so that you will
    not deviate from the path.

7   Most of those who like to show off their talents or
    want to gain advantage over others end up in fail-
    ure. Therefore, don't turn your back on other peo-
    ple's advice simply because you feel you are better
    educated, better informed, or more capable.
    Otherwise, your education and intelligence will
    only foster arrogance, hamper your practice, and
    make it more difficult for you to be in accord with
    Buddhadharma. There is an old saying: "Humility
    gains; arrogance losses." The more talented and
    capable you are, the more humble you should be.
    Such is a reflection of true wisdom.

8   Everyday when beating the evening drum, we ought
    to recite the following stanza in our minds: "Get
    public work done, public work be done. Put public
    work before private affairs." This recitation is to
    remind us that we should not let others do public
    duties while we ourselves concentrate only on our
    own practice (whether reciting the Buddha's name
    or the sutras, or performing prostration, they are
    all private affairs). If a practitioner focuses only on
    private affairs instead of vowing to work for the
    benefit of others, he/she is still clinging tightly to

the sense of "self" and can never attain liberation.
On the other hand, if a practitioner is dedicated to
the monastery, is compassionate to all beings while
providing them with expedient guidance for practice, he/she will be filled with dharmic joy. Thus,
in practicing altruism, you can unfold the wisdom
immanent in your mind and accumulate merits
along the way. This is called the dual practice
toward gaining both merit and wisdom.

9   Do not keep on clinging to the sense of "self."
Otherwise, you will continue to drift within the
five *kasaya* periods of impurity and among the six
divisions of rebirth, with no hope of escaping.

10   If you succumb to your physical desires and insist
on having good food and lavish clothing, all these
attachments are reflections of your greediness.

11   We practitioners should not plan on being vener-
ated. If we do, we are greedy and are still attached
the "form of self." Be humble and courteous so that
we can eliminate our attachment to the "form of
self." If we walk the path according to the wisdom
of ordinariness, we are practicing to attain *"sila,
samadhi,* and *prajna* (precepts, perfect absorption,
and wisdom)."

12 More often than not, we are unaware of our own attachments. The results of such attachments will naturally surface when conditions are ripe. These results are our "karmic obstructions." Over the eons, all of us have accumulated immeasurable and illimitable negative karma. If we do not grad-ually reduce them through diligent practice, they will appear at our deathbed. So, at that crucial moment, whatever you crave for or are attached to will come forth to distract you. Without adequate self-control, you will be swayed easily by these distractions and remain fluctuating in the cycle of birth and death. If you crave for even a blade of grass in this world, you will be reborn into it and remain in samsara. A blade of grass symbolizes an idea, and an idea stands for one cycle of birth and death. So you see, the power of our minds is immeasurable. Without the guidance of right mindfulness, we will follow the fluctuation of our own karma without even realizing it. Thus, many that appear to be practicing solemnly are in fact mostly absorbed in their illusive and erroneous thoughts.

13 The purpose of listening to the sermons is to prac-tice the methods expounded in order to rectify misconduct and eradicate karma. Don't continue to follow illusive ideas and clutch on to your own "egotistic views." Neither should you keep making

distinctions between "self and others," nor hold on to your habitual tendencies of gossiping and making judgments. Remember to recite the name of the Buddha as often as possible!

14 You can neither deliver sentient beings by words nor preach the Dharma by offerings. What you should do is to practice diligently and attain a stage where you can impress and convert others without deliberate efforts. Only by then will you be able to deliver other beings.

.6.

On Calming the Mind

1   About going into seclusion for practice: is it your
     mind or is it your body that needs to be secluded?
     If the former, then your mind is the place where
     your can practice and your body of temporary
     fusion of the four elements is spacious enough for
     the purpose. But if your mind is dispersed and
     your body craves for material comforts, it doesn't
     matter how spacious the place is, it will not be
     large enough to contain your distracted mind
     ruled by physical desires.

2   People nowadays are different from those of the
     old days. If the latter were one hundred percent
     devoted to practice, the former is only ten.

3   How to stabilize the mind during practice? We can
     start by not engaging our minds in whatever cir-
     cumstances we run into while staying unfettered
     whether at rest or in action. But what is the mind?
     As the mind alights on nothing and fills the illimit-
     able void of the universe, where can we find it?

Those fettered by attachments are not our real minds; they are ordinary, physical minds defiled by karmic forces and secular apprehensions.

4 In everyone's mind, there are always two forces-- the moral and the evil--struggling against each other. Unfortunately, the latter always prevails. When the moral one says: "I am good," the evil one will respond: "No! No! You are evil, I am good!" The "evil" force is aggressive and likes to show off. Without practice to reinforce the moral force, the evil one will easily prevail thereby creating karmic obstructions for us. Thus, it is said (in the *Scripture Concerning Ti-ts'ang's Fundamental Promises*) that: "The incipience of our ideas are all sinful and destructive." We should all practice diligently in order to nurture the good seeds. Continue to sow the seeds of noble ideas and eradicate the bad ones poisoned by our greed, anger, and ignorance. If we do, these good seeds will naturally sprout when we face adversities and present us with right mindfulness to ward off the temptation of evil ideas.

5 Are you afraid? If you are free of fear, your mind is calm; if not, it is restless. Fear springs up when your mind becomes dispersed; you fear because you are unable to compose yourself. Accumulated fear inevitably generates vexations; and a restless mind will impede determination in practice.

6   Relinquish all your attachments! If you can do
    that, you have already attained a certain stage in
    your practice. Practice to always be free of anxiety
    and impediments lest any idea of attachment
    should distract you at your deathbed and confine
    you to the cycle of rebirths.

7   Nothing is more important than escaping the cycle
    of birth and death! Since everything in this world
    is but phantasm and magical delusion, why cling
    to, or worry about, it? Learn to let go! Whatever
    others do, it's not your concern. Do not let every-
    thing hang over your head thus creates vexations
    for yourself. Otherwise, you will be constantly
    under the whims of others and there will be no
    hope of your escaping the six divisions of rebirth.

8   Our vexation has no real substance. It comes and
    goes like the wind, leaving no trace and nothing to
    hold on to. Even so, as long as we are vexed, we
    can never feel quite at ease. The purpose of prac-
    tice is to untie our minds from all impediments,
    particularly the notion of "who I am, what I am
    doing" (so that our minds won't be bridled by our
    sense of self).

9   "Let go of all attachments" is not just a slogan; you
    should carry it out in your daily activities, be it
    walking, staying, sitting, or sleeping. For example,

if you recite the name of the Buddha solemnly with an unfettered mind to the extent that right mindfulness comes forth to guide you when you die and you don't suffer from the pain of parting with loved ones, then you have genuinely "let go of all attachments." You should know that even an inkling of attachment is powerful enough to confine you to the cycle of birth and death. We are all born into this world with boundless karmic obstructions accumulated in our previous lives. Instead of adding more negative karma through incessant pursuit of good food, lavish clothing, and cozy housing, we should learn and practice Buddhadharma. Otherwise, we would still be trapped in the old path of rebirths.

10   There is no need to quest for a long life. If you do not recognize the need of liberation and the meaning of practice, the longer you live the more time you would have to accumulate karmic obstructions. Even if you live to be two hundred, you still can't avoid falling back to the cycle of birth and death. This physical body of ours is by no means permanent; it will decay and eventually perish. Therefore, we should relinquish our attachments to our body and practice to bring forth the essence of our minds, which is our intrinsic nature and is above birth and death.

.7.

On Forbearance

1 Be patient and tolerant when under attack or
   criticism. Even when falsely accused, feel grateful
   for the opportunity to practice "forbearance." "No
   attainment in practice is possible without forbearance." Those who can bear insult without resentment have attained genuine wisdom.

2 Forbearance does not mean that you should keep
   reminding yourself "I have to tolerate this," or feel
   "I am being patient." If such reminders are necessary, you are still clinging to the "form" of forbearance. Practice to the extent that external circumstances will have no bearing on either your emotions or your mind. For example, when people
   reprimand you, you do not feel being reproached.
   This is "formless," hence genuine, forbearance.

3 You should express your repentance when others
   insist that you are wrong, even though you might
   be in the right. It is to acquire such forbearance
   that we practice.

4   Be tolerant even when others blame us for things they have messed up. Regard it as a good opportunity to practice "forbearance" and "selflessness."

5   Do not regard those who attack, criticize, or reprimand us as evil. From the perspective of practice, they are providing us with adverse conditions that can help our endeavors. Those who know how to transform circumstances will use these opportunities to exercise forbearance and attain a higher stage in their practice. They will also feel grateful because these adversities are assets upon which they can depend to be reborn in the Pure Land. (Therefore, when facing blame, criticism, or accusation, you should) accept it and endure it instead of weeping about it. Otherwise, you are just being foolish!

6   Only by bearing all distresses can you expect to make progress in practice. Repent to your accuser even though you are in the right. If you were able to do this, you would have attained a certain level in practice.

7   If we can tolerate insults, bullying, and being taken advantage of without seeking retribution or being vexed, not only will we eradicate our karmic obstructions but we also will attain instant peace of the mind. And as we are free of vexations, our merits and wisdom will grow.

8   Forbearance is the foundation of practice and the
      most important precept. It is the largest source of
      merit. Those who can practice forbearance will
      enjoy the greatest blessed rewards. Forbearance
      will also help to strengthen self-control, alleviate
      karmic obstructions, and unfold wisdom.

9   Most people are unwilling to be taken advantage of
      or to acknowledge that they are in the wrong.
      Thus, they constantly argue rights from wrongs,
      bitterly pointing fingers at others, even using
      words sharp as knives when making their accusa-
      tions. We monastic practitioners, with our practice
      based on forbearance and compassion, should act
      differently. Whatever the nature of the circum-
      stances we come across, however unmistakably
      unreasonable, we should invariably handle them
      with gentleness and compassion. Try to tolerate
      everything and practice forbearance against all
      adverse circumstances. This is the true virtue of
      monastic practitioners.

10   In the course of seeking guidance, we should not
      expect to be treated well or gain any advantage.
      Rather, try to learn through adverse conditions. If
      you won't tolerate being taken advantage of, you
      won't learn anything. Hence, "forbearance" is of
      utmost importance. We should endure not only
      physical hardships but also challenges of all sorts.

For example, when others resent us, not only should we bear no hard feelings but we also should foster good affinity by reciting "Amitabha Buddha" for them. Only those who practice forbearance can expect to have their wisdom fully unfold.

11 The minds of monastic practitioners should be free of anger and resentment. The worse people treat us, the more compassionate we should be in our attempt to deliver them. Do not harbor resentment or take revenge, as any lay people would.

12 The monastery is a place where people from all different places come for practice, so everyone here has his/her own unique character. We have to adapt to this environment, not vise versa. For all we know, it is impossible to ask even our own parents or siblings, not to mention people from different places, to accommodate us. Therefore, learn tolerance and humbleness so that our minds can settle and our practice can be on the right track.

13 Monastic practice is quite different from lay practice. In the monastery, instead of arguing right or wrong with your master, you have to accept all instructions. If you can be so patient and tolerant, your attachment to the "form of self" will be expelled gradually.

14 If someone finds faults with us, we should remind ourselves: "This is a good chance to exercise for-bearance and make progress in practice." So, instead of blaming others, we should reflect upon ourselves. Remember, no matter how we feel, our sentiments are nothing but distinctions made by our minds.

.8.

On Gossiping

1   Those who like to gossip are bound to create nega-
    tive karma through their words. They are also
    "troublemakers."

2   Avert words so as to shun misdeeds. When you do
    speak, make it to the point and cut all unnecessary
    remarks.

3   Do not gossip. Gossip leads to failure; gossip makes
    people feel restless.

4   Before criticizing others, consult your mind first.

5   Don't keep finding fault with, or making comments
    about, others. As soon as you utter one word, you
    are in the wrong and are creating negative karma
    of words. Therefore, it is very important for prac-
    titioners to be watchful of what they say.

6   Through their words, some people can easily make
    others feel vexed or baffled, not knowing what to

do. Unfortunately, these same people are also prone to insist that others comply with their wishes, though they themselves never listen to others. These people are likely to become deluded and vexed, and are difficult to be liberated.

7   Be watchful of your own mind all the time: curb all greedy aspirations and unnecessary chattering. There are enough bad seeds to confine you in the cycle of rebirths, do not plant more. Discuss Buddhadharma if any conversation is necessary and vow to be reborn in the Pure Land.

8   When you are vexed, do not talk to one person after another. The more you talk, the more trouble you will cause. You might as well use the time to perform prostration. This will alleviate your karmic obstructions thereby reduce your vexations.

9   Those who praise and flatter us are not good teachers. On the contrary, those who criticize us, be it right or wrong, can truly help us in our practice. When reproaching us, the latter are providing us with chances to reflect on ourselves and strengthen our practice. So when we are reprimanded, not only should we feel ashamed and repent our karma, but we also should reaffirm our vows and practice even more diligently. Only by so doing can we expect to make progress in our practice.

10   "Do not detest those whom others detest, or criti-
     cize those whom others criticize." When others
     foster negative affinities, do not follow. You should
     be able to master your own mind and make inde-
     pendent judgments so as to foster good affinities
     with others, which is essential because "before
     attaining buddhahood, be sure to foster good
     karmic affinity with people."

11   To find fault with others and talk about it is a
     sinister act in itself; it is also an indication of an
     impure mind. Your mind will become more com-
     posed and unfettered if you get rid of the habit of
     differentiating pleasant circumstances from the
     bad. Therefore, keep it to yourself when you see
     anything immoral or anybody breaching the
     Dharma. Do not expose them, nor feel any aver-
     sion. "With your mind in a pure state, you will be
     free of vexations." This also indicates the potency
     of your practice.

12   From the perspective of practice, the major prob-
     lem of criticizing others is not "whether he is in
     fact wrong and I am right," but the fact that our
     ears and eyes are already making judgments and
     our minds are closed to everything but our own
     perceptions. Further, we are creating negative
     karma through the incipience of our ideas and
     depriving ourselves of merits. Therefore, our six

sensual organs are like six thieves, and the purpose of practice is to prevent them from wildly pursuing the sense objects so that we can close the door to vexation. We should train our ears not to crave for pleasant melodies; eyes, agreeable surroundings; nose, fragrance; mouth, tasty food; and train our minds to be free of discrimination. Then we can concentrate on reciting the Buddha's name and the sutras, performing prostration, sitting meditation, and other practices that will liberate us from the cycle of birth and death. If we keep up these practices, how could we have the time and the mood to pursue external distractions, or to comment on how others behave?

13 If you criticize others and your mind is disturbed or vexed by it, you would have no one but yourself to blame. Do not be judgmental of what others do: be tolerant. Then, not only will you enjoy peace of mind but will avoid creating negative karma through your words. This is the first and utmost important principle in practice. Remember: "Act according to (rather than against) circumstances, forbear everything, then enjoy peace of mind." This is the best antidote for a troubled mind.

14 Don't say that there are good people and evil ones. All judgments are but distinctions made by our minds. To those who really know how to practice, all sentient beings are helpful mentors.

15   When somebody tries to harm us, we should think:
     "It must be because I have done him harm in pre-
     vious lives. I should stop this vicious cycle of bad
     karmic affinity and try to liberate him as well."
     Everything that happens, no matter how insignifi-
     cant, has a cause.

16   Some people always look around and act mysteri-
     ously when talking to others. Those who saw such
     behavior might think he/she was speaking ill of
     somebody, which is not necessarily true. Therefore,
     we should be ourselves in whatever we do lest we
     should create unnecessary misunderstandings.

.9.

On Work Ethics

1   Whatever you do, do it willingly and joyfully; otherwise, your wisdom can not grow.

2   Do whatever needs to be done, irrespective of whose responsibility it is. As long as you do it willingly, you will earn merits for yourself. Do not criticize others for not doing their jobs. Bad-mouthing will only create negative karma. Remember, you are working for no one else but yourself in order to eradicate your karmic obstructions.

3   Think (and plan) carefully in whatever you do and be your own master. Do not follow blindly what others say or do, make your own judgments. Practice means cultivating wisdom through the tasks we perform and the mistakes we make.

4   Perform your monastic assignments dutifully. If you simply want to enjoy a good life and neglect

your duty, your merits accumulated in previous lives will soon be used up. By then, you will be under the full swing of your karmic obstructions and it will naturally be difficult for you to hold on and continue your practice in the monastery.

5   Concentrate on your assignments and do your best. Do not try your hands on everything and end up doing nothing well.

6   Through carrying out daily chores in the temple, we may discipline our minds to become sharp and deft. The way a person performs his/her duties reflects the degree of dedication and concentration of his/her mind. Those who carry out their tasks with an undivided mind can also concentrate on their practice. That's why we should try to comprehend the essence of practice through performing monastic duties. Thus, when you carry out your assignments with utmost sincerity and concentration, your mind will be as pure and clean as the bright moon, and your wisdom will fully unfold. By then, you will know clearly as to what needs to be done or where has to be cleaned, even a grain of dust on the floor will not escape your eyes. As everything becomes apparent and crystal clear, you will not feel bewildered at the

tasks assigned to you. Such a state indicates the revelation of wisdom.

7   Cheerfully accept instructions and advice. For example, the Master might ask you to wipe again the chair you just cleaned. Your spontaneous reaction might be: "Why? It is clean enough!" If so, you still react like a lay person rather than a practitioner, and vexations will arise. As a practitioner's mind is straightforward, you should just answer: "Fine, I'll wipe it again." This will test your proficiency in practice and gives you an opportunity to train your mind.

8   In addition to perseverance, an attitude of "non-attachment" is also necessary to do a job well. "Non-attachment" does not mean indifference or carelessness, but rather you should do your best and not worry about the results. If your mind lingers on the task after it is done, it is a sign of attachment. Such attachment will obscure your wisdom, generate vexation, and even spoil your accomplishment.

9   Be patient in performing all your tasks. For example, when you are sweeping the floor, not only should you clean the floor but also purify your mind. You can recite the name of the

Buddha while working. Don't let your mind become slack or diffused. Practice disciplining your mind through work so as to purify your deeds, words, and thoughts.

10 Be patient while working. Also, recite the Buddha's name and free your mind from vexations. By so doing, you will naturally attain a certain level in your practice.

11 "Treat everything of the monastery with care, as if protecting your own eyes." Plan carefully before taking any action, rather than doing it at will and carelessly. Use the most proper and flawless way to take care of the possessions and affairs of the monastery.

12 Do your best on your daily chores and practice diligently with an undivided mind. Were you able to do so, even sweeping the floor can lead to enlightenment.

13 Work can train our minds to concentrate and make our reactions deft. Therefore, it's better that we have something to do lest we should be overrun by erroneous and illusive ideas and waste our life in vain.

14   "Don't think too much" does not mean that you should not use your head and make plans when carrying out a task, but that you should not dwell on it once the job is done. Lingering not on past successes or failures lest your vexations should increase.

15   Don't be stubborn and insist on a certain way of doing things or cling to any specific principle; flow with circumstances! For example, when someone does you a favor, if you feel uncomfortable because you either think you are unworthy or fear it might cost you some merits, then you are rigidly clinging to a principle. In fact, if you wish others to gain merits, you yourself have to acquire abundant merits and wisdom, and attained an impeccable level in your practice. Only by then can you persuade others to follow you, to plant the field of blessings thereby increase their positive affinity with Buddhism. And such efforts are in accord with the bodhisattva vow that quests for self-elevation while benefiting others.

16   At times, those who are in responsible positions in the monastery may reprimand us or correct our mistakes. They do so because they care about us. Regard them as our valuable mentors; don't be upset or be vexed upon hearing any reproach.

17 Put the Master's words into practice: recite the name of the Buddha while carrying out your daily chores about the temple; get rid of your clinging to both "the sense of self" and "the Dharma." By so doing, you can gradually unfold your wisdom. However, wisdom is formless and colorless; you might not even realize that it has unfolded. But when it does, you can naturally figure out the most adroit and flawless way to handle any problem that emerges.

18 You should incorporate recitation into your daily routines, i.e. recite the Buddha's name while working to the extent that your mind becomes tranquil and untainted, and you can hear distinctly every word you recite. "Recite with the essence of your mind and listen with the same" until the mind is "undivided and unperturbed."

19 Recite the name of the Buddha with an undi-vided mind. But when you concentrate on your work and are free of illusive thoughts, your mind is also undivided. In that state, you would have no thought but how to benefit others and whatever you do would be based on lovingkindness and compassion; also all your understandings would naturally be right views hence your mind a buddha-mind.

20 Work can help discipline and keep our minds from being distracted and dispersed. Therefore, to monastic practitioners, the meaning of work is not the same as that to lay people because their inspiration and goal are not the same. Lay people work to earn profit, monastic practitioners to enhance their practice. Maybe there seems not much difference as monks/nuns, like lay people, also need three meals a day along with proper clothing and housing, but the essence is completely different.

21 How can we carry out a task successfully? It requires complete cooperation and communication among all involved. It won't work if someone within a group would only give orders. For example, when working on a garden, if someone is unfamiliar with the task, those who do should show him how to do it. Otherwise, not only things can't get done, animosity may be generated within the group.

22 Monastic practitioners ought to be merciful and compassionate. Do not try to command people according to lay principles. Put the Dharma into practice so that, by our virtue, we can convert other sentient beings naturally.

23 "Don't do anything that is immoral, and do all things that are right." Practitioners should unconditionally do whatever would benefit other beings. And, instead of being resentful, endure all hardships with a pure and joyful mind. Fill your heart with senses of lovingkindness, compassion, joy, and equanimity and carry out your daily tasks with a *bodhi* mind. Keep on these practices and you will eventually comprehend their true virtue and your wisdom will unfold.

24 Instead of criticizing others, we should try our best to do things others would not do, or to complete tasks others could not finish. Otherwise, we would be acting like a lay person.

25 "Alms come from the ten directions (i.e. different places) should be returned to the ten directions." People from the ten directions offer alms to the temple, believing they are planting the field of merit. We who receive such alms should practice diligently so that their offerings would not be given in vain. Then, we should transfer our merits acquired through practice to all beings of the ten directions. By such transfer of merits, we should wish to repay the grace of our parents, of all beings, of the state,

and of the *triratna* (Buddha, Dharma, and *Sangha*) and to relieve the suffering of those in the three evil divisions of rebirth (beasts, hell, and hungry ghosts), and hope that all beings can escape misery and attain happiness.

26 As a lay practitioner working in the secular world, you should always keep your promises, avoid greediness, and do your best in all endeavors. If you are devoted to your tasks, your supervisor will hold you in high regard. It is the same with being a Buddhist: if you truly believe in the Buddha, the Buddha will bless you.

.10.

On Habitual Patterns

1   Good-natured, even-tempered people are more accommodating and can get along with others wherever they go. However, being "accommodating" does not suggest that we should comply with whatever others say. Rather, we should keep a clear head as to the nature of the situation and use our own judgement. When things contradict the Dharma, (instead of going along,) we should stick to our own principles.

2   People may have bad habits, but they are not necessarily evil. Everyone is under the influence of varying degrees of habitual tendencies hence wrongdoing is inevitable. As long as the wrongdoer is willing to repent and rectify his/her misconduct, be as tolerant and forgiving as possible. There is no need to regard him/her as evil.

3   A little story: A had a habit of spitting all over the places and B tended to be suspicious. One day A spit in front of B. B considered it an insult and

started a brawl. C knew about the habits of these two and came to mediate. Both knew they had been wrong and were determined to change. In the end, A stopped spitting and B overcame his suspiciousness.

4   Some people are in the habit of criticizing others whenever they open their mouth, even though they do not do it intentionally, nor do they realize that they are indeed "gossiping." This kind of habitual pattern is the result of continual repetition through the eons.

5   Another story: There were two people, one is beautiful, the other ugly. The latter realized her deficiency and tried to compensate by using heavy make-up. The effect, however, was quite the opposite. She might as well let it be.

6   We can not expect someone to govern a nation well if he can not even handle his own family affairs. Likewise, there is a sequence according to which we should proceed our practice. First of all, we should get rid of our negative habitual patterns as well as all the bad seeds of delusion and vexation. Only by then will we be capable of leading the laity in practice and of converting other beings.

7   The greatest of our habitual tendencies caused by delusion is that we only see the mistakes of others, but seldom reflect on the shortcomings of our own.

8   Due to a lack of trials through hardships, those growing up under protective parents are most likely to become immature and weak in character. On the other hand, those who have to fight for a living tend to be more courageous and capable. For example, the little monkeys held closely by their mothers might be smothered while those who live independently in the jungles survive well. This is also true in our practice: the best conditions for practice are adverse conditions. That's why those who are most proficient in forbearance usually have experienced numerous circumstances that require their utmost tolerance. Therefore, adverse conditions should be regarded as challenging components aiding our practice.

9   We practitioners should not allow old habits and set patterns to take charge of our lives. If we do, not only will we be unable to make any progress in practice, but we also will create negative karma through our words. Remember, "What you eat feed yourself only. Similarly, the matter of your own birth and death can only be taken care of by yourself." Nobody--not your loving family members or

even your son--can die (or live) for you. The only way you can learn how to walk the path to the Pure Land is through diligent recitation of the Buddha's name to the extent that you yourself can see clearly the path of birth and death.

.11.

On a Simple Life

1   Nowadays, everybody, either living at home or in the monastery, enjoys a very comfortable life. Unfortunately, this is not necessarily a blessing as it can easily lead to a degenerated and disorganized lifestyle and bring about calamity. If you further indulge yourself in the pursuit of sensual passions hence spoil this body of yours, you are also more likely to suffer from all sorts of disease.

2   In order to practice, you have to relinquish your attachments to physical gratification and live a simple life. If you enjoy and are contented with plain food and clothing, you will be happy all the time. On the other hand, if you pay too much attention to the qualities of food, clothing, and housing, etc., then you will be no different from a lay person. Only by relinquishing all your attachments to physical satisfaction can you expect to eliminate your greed, anger and ignorance. As you know, a lavish lifestyle will inevitably induce more desire and arouse greediness in you. In due

course, the five *skandhas* (form, sensation, perception, volition, and consciousness) will have a
firm grip of both your body and your mind. And
as you immerse yourself in these impurities, you
can never feel free. Thus, "relinquishing attachments to the body" should begin by simplifying
your clothing, food, and living conditions.

3   Practice should begin with consuming only "plain
food and clothing." Unfortunately, people nowadays (practitioners included) tend to pay a great
deal of attention to what they eat or wear and
often preoccupy themselves all day long for such
pursuits. As a result, practitioners not only can
not reduce their negative karma, but their merits
and wisdom accumulated in previous lives will be
drained. Then, their karmic obstructions will
naturally come forth.

4   What is the essence of "simple food and clothing?" It certainly doesn't mean that you should
give up food or clothes. Rather, just feed yourself
without craving the taste and keep yourself warm
without pursuing a lavish style. Also, you should
get enough sleep so as to be energetic, but do not
oversleep lest you feel slumberous. If you insist on
the extremes of no food or sleep thereby spoiling
your health and feeling even less at ease in the
monastery, it will also spoil your efforts of leaving
home for practice.

5   People are often driven blindly by their sensual
     desires. For example, some people are willing to
     kill just to satisfy their palate, not knowing they
     might be eating the flesh of their relatives from
     previous lives. Besides, according to the law of
     karma, you have to repay in full everything you
     do. Though you have acquired human existence
     in this life, you are still confined to the vicious
     cycle of demanding and repaying the debts from
     previous lives. If you do not practice diligently in
     search for a way out, you will be forever impris-
     oned in this cycle of rebirths.

6   Do not crave for more than you actually need. All
     you require is enough to sustain your life. If you
     eat more just because there is plenty available, it
     only reflects the greediness of your mind.
     However, don't deliberately eat less and starve
     yourself, for this is also a form of attachment.
     How much you should eat depends on how much
     you need. Have enough food, but make no distinc-
     tion of taste.

7   Eat only to sustain your life. If you indulge your-
     self in the pursuit of satisfying your palate, you
     are enslaved by your mouth. It not only will
     increase the burden of your digestive system, but
     also will increase your sense of illusion, disper-
     sion, and attachment. Life should be simple: eat so

that you won't starve and wear so that you can cover yourself and keep warm; that's sufficient.

8   If you are used to living lavishly and being waited on, you can easily become arrogant. Also, the smarter you are, the stronger your sense of "self" will be. Without using Buddhadharma as an antidote to reflect on yourself thereby learn to repent and be humble, it will be very difficult for you to break out of the confinement of the form of "self."

9   Food, clothing, and housing are necessary to sustain our lives, but avoid consuming more than the basics. If you pursue a lavish lifestyle instead of restraining your sensual passions, you not only will be unable to reduce your negative karma, but will add more to it thus generate bitter fruits for yourself.

10   While eating, ponder gratefully, "Where does the food come from and how does it get here?" Introspect: "Have I practiced diligently to deserve this food?" Without a sense of appreciation, even a casual comment such as "the food tastes awful" will cost you some merit.

11   If, instead of enduring hardships and relinquishing your desires, you insist on eating well and

living comfortably, why bother leaving home for practice? What differences are there between you and any layman? We monastic practitioners should not pay too much attention on satisfying our sensual desires. As long as the food is edible and sufficient, do not insist on good flavor. Only through such practice can we expect to relinquish our desires and unfold our wisdom.

12 Working in the kitchen of the monastery is following the path of Bodhisattva Samantabhadra. In fact, many great bodhisattvas such as Avalokitesvara and Manjusri have practiced asceticism through working in the kitchen. The kitchen is a place where you can easily either amass or waste away your merits. Do not casually throw away edible food or leftovers lest you should bear the consequences, such as to be reborn as a chicken, duck, pig, or dog and all you can eat are leftovers or spoiled food.

13 Recite silently before each meal: "I vow to annihilate all the vice, to practice all the virtue, and to deliver all sentient beings." To annihilate all the "vice" means eradicating all sinister thoughts at their incipience. For example, picking the better part from a dish reflects clearly a sense of "discrimination" and "covetousness." Thoughts of this nature are sinister and should be eliminated.

14 Once we leave home for practice, the world is our home. We should be able to practice anywhere we are, so why look for any particular place? What matters is our resolve, not a specific type of monastery that caters to our wish. With resolve, we can feel at home and make progress in our practice even only residing in a bamboo shelter in the woods. Our minds will be stable as long as we have the resolve to overcome any and all obstacles. With determination and an unwavering mind, we can practice wherever we are.

15 Before plunging into any type of ascetic practice such as never lying down to sleep, one has to start with relinquishing the pursuit of physical gratification. After you are free of sensual passions as well as of the defilement of greed, anger, and ignorance, your illusive ideas will naturally diminish. At that stage, you can venture into the more advanced steps in Zen practice.

16 This world is nothing but our temporary residence. Everything in this world is like a phantasm or a magical delusion, as unreal as things in our dream or in a drama. Do not mistake the seeming for the being thereby long for anything in this world. Relinquish all attachments, practice reciting the name of the Buddha, and vow to be reborn in the Pure Land. Only Amitabha Buddha

is our ultimate refuge and the Pure Land our true homeland.

.12.

On the Foul Body

1   We are not born with material wealth, nor can we, or mega-millionairs for that matter, bring our assets along when we die. The only thing that will follow us through all lives is our own karma. So why waste valuable time pursuing material wealth? We should grasp the little time we have in human existence and start practicing as early as possible.

2   Relinquish all attachments to this foul body! The most important goal for practice is to liberate our minds, not to tend to the desires of our physical body and let it control our lives. Also, remember not to cling to the idea of attainment during practice. Whatever can be attained will vanish eventually, hence is not genuinely unmovable, as is our intrinsic nature.

3   Our body, just like a house, will eventually decay; however hard we try to mend it, it can never be free of problems. Let go of excessive concern

about this body, do not be too fastidious about it; after all, it is only a phantasm. What we should do is to make the best use of this "illusive" body for "real" practice.

4   This foul body is just a temporary residence for us. Unfortunately, we all become strongly attached to it, and our greediness that arises due to our incessant pursuits to satisfy its carvings has in turn created immeasurable negative karma for us.

5   Diseases are inevitable with this illusory body of ours, but they are not as perilous as the ailments of delusion, greed, anger, and ignorance. The latter will keep us in the cycle of rebirths if we do not find a cure. The most effective prescription is reciting "Amitabha Buddha," and retaining right mindfulness at our deathbed is crucial. At that critical moment, if we can recite "Amitabha Buddha" distinctly and steadily, by the mercy of the Buddha we will be able to transcend the six divisions of rebirth. Otherwise, with our con-sciousness inverted, where will we end up after we die?

6   Very few people can enjoy blessed rewards throughout their lives. The extent of rewards you can enjoy is proportional to the degree of hard-ships you endure.

7   Master Hsu Yun used to live a very simple life. He wore clothes with multi-layered patches and could not even count on food for the next meal. But such hardships did not deter him from diligent practice. He has only one goal in mind: to be liberated from the cycle of birth and death.

8   If we wreck anything because of our carelessness, we are at fault and have to take the consequences.

9   Be careful on what you do for nothing is beyond the law of karma; even things as trivial as throwing away edible food or letting it spoil will have their consequences. Nobody can take the consequences for what you do, and there is no escape from the law of karma. "What you eat feed yourself only. Similarly, the matter of your own birth and death can only be taken care of by yourself."

10   Handle with care those papers printed or written with words. It would be better to burn them (than throw them into the garbage dump). This is also a virtue.

11   Practice relinquishing the attachments of your sense organs to the six *gunas* (sense objects). Otherwise, the thing you crave for will appear at your deathbed to distract you. If it prevails and your mind is inverted, you will remain in the

cycle of rebirths. Practice relinquishing all your discriminations between self and others and your judgements of right or wrong. Then, when you are breathing your last, this practice will help you transcend your karmic obstructions and the cycle of birth and death.

12 Do not mistake this physical form of ours as the real "self." It is nothing but a temporary and illusive outer case bearing our karma. The real "self" is our "*tathata*," or buddha-nature immanent within our minds, which can neither be born nor be destroyed (i.e. permanent, transcending birth and death). Therefore, we should, through diligent practice, retrieve this intrinsic nature and confront everything with our buddha-mind.

13 Monastic practitioners should concentrate on practice; nothing else should distract their attention. Lay people who do not realize the need for practice are living in inverted dreams, their fettered mind bugged by incessant vexations. They dream not only in their sleep but also while they are awake. Time passes as they watch their lives slip by, like watching a movie. To them, life is nothing but a longer dream.

14 It is not easy or just by coincidence that we
acquire this human existence. Seize this opportunity and practice diligently so as to eradicate our
sense of greed and free ourselves from the agony
of birth, aging, disease, and death, hence the
cycle of rebirths. With this human existence, we
can either practice to attain buddhahood or
bodhisattvahood, or generate negative karma that
would lead to rebirth in the three evil divisions
(beasts, hungry ghosts, and hell). Whether we
will ascend or descend within the ten dharma
realms depends on our conduct in this human
rebirth. Therefore, human existence is a crucial
turning point that should not be taken lightly, nor
be wasted in vain.

.13.

On the Pure Land

1   Where, exactly, is the Pure Land? It is immanent within yonr mind. As long as you are free of worries and vexations, your mind is the land of equanimity hence the Pure Land.

2   When reciting the name of the Buddha, pronounce each word distinctly with full concentration. Further, vow to be reborn in the Pure Land so as to escape this bitter prison of samsara.

3   "When the mind is pure, the buddha-land is also pure." Practice recitation diligently to the extent that the mind is pure, clear, and unfettered by vexations or illusive thoughts. When you attain such a state, this world is the Pure Land and your mind the kingdom of Amitabha Buddha.

4   Within the limitless void, a world resembles a grain of sand. If there are as many worlds as there are grains of sand in the Ganges, and if all beings of these worlds are willing to recite the

Buddha's name, they can all be reborn in the Pure Land.

5   An important prerequisite to be reborn in the Pure Land is to relinquish all worldly concerns. One can only be reborn in the Pure Land without the encumbrances and entanglements of this world.

6   If our minds are composed and stable, we are naturally free of vexations. We can live every day with a pure mind and good spirit, crave for nothing but live according to circumstances, and our hearts will be filled with joy and bliss. Such is the state of the Pure Land. So why quest elsewhere when the Pure Land is immanent within our minds? On the other hand, if your mind is unsettling and disgruntling, you will become vexed easily and you will feel restless wherever you are.

7   Practice recitation to the extent that your mind becomes absolutely pure and clear, and you will be reborn through the lotus into the Pure Land. Those who are born through the physical bodies of their parents will remain in the cycle of birth and death.

8   Do not pray for the divine manifestation of buddhas and/or bodhisattvas at your deathbed.

Such revelations are most likely to be illusions. What you should do is to recite the name of the Buddha with a mind pure and free of appeals. Then, whatever is manifested in your mind will be genuine revelation.

9   There are limits to the merits we can enjoy in this world. But the blessings we attain through practice will invigorate our buddha-nature, unfold our wisdom, and help us retrieve our true nature. It is by no means easy to become monastic practitioners, as we have to endure immeasurable hardships. But such endurance will help us remove the massive karmic obstructions we have accumulated through the eons. Only by so doing will we be able to eradicate all our negative karma, be reborn in the Pure Land, and ultimately attain buddhahood.

10   (At dusk, we recite the following stanza:) "The day is drawing to an end and our lives are cutting short accordingly. Just like the fishes in a drying pond, how much joy can there be?" Indeed, we do not realize that our lives are drawing closer to an end each day, just like the fishes in a drying pond that are still swimming happily, not realizing their imminent extinction. We just live one day after another, do not know where we are going after we die. Therefore, we should constantly

remind ourselves not to lessen our vigilance. Practice diligently so that we can be reborn in the Pure Land.

11 A diligent practitioner is just like an old farmer who tills in the field all day and can joyfully rest at home after the sun goes down. The Pure Land is his ultimate home and resting-place.

12 We monastic practitioners should not be afraid of death because there is the Pure Land to look forward to. We should also attain the level in our practice at which we can easily untie our minds from all worldly concerns and can resolve all difficulties with a simple change of perception.

13 A snap of thought takes 90 *ksana* (of time), and there are 900 births and deaths within a *ksana*. Hence, within the time of a snap of thought, there are 81,000 births and deaths. At the critical moment of our last breath, even only one snap of thought (other than the wish to be reborn in the Pure Land) arises to distract us, we will be unable to escape the cycle of birth and death. Thus, the last snap of thought before we die is of utmost importance! What kind of thought will flash through our minds depends on the state of our minds at that instant. If our minds are completely pure and we are making no distinction among the

forms of self, others, sentient beings, and life, we will be reborn in the Pure Land.

14   Where is the Pure Land? You have to begin your search through purifying your own mind. If your mind is unfettered by worldly distractions and delusion, and is absolutely pure and clear, then your mind itself is the Pure Land. So there is no need to keep questing "where is the Pure Land?" If you continue to have such an illusive idea of pursuit, you are still defiled by greed, anger, and ignorance. Do not cling to the idea that there is indeed a Pure Land somewhere out there. In fact, the Pure Land is immanent in your mind and can only be brought out through diligent practice. As an old stanza makes it clear: "Do not search afar for the Buddha because the Buddha is right there at the Spirit Vulture Peak, and the Peak within your mind. Everyone has a pagoda under the Spirit Vulture Peak within his/her mind, under which he/she can practice to attain buddhahood." It will be a total mistake to search for the Buddha outside our minds. If we practice by training our minds, we can eventually reach the Pure Land.

DEDICATION OF MERIT

May the merit and virtue
accrued from this work
adorn Amitabha Buddha's Pure Land,
repay the four great kindnesses above,
and relieve the suffering of
those on the three paths below.

May those who see or hear of these efforts
generate Bodhi-mind,
spend their lives devoted to the Buddha Dharma,
and finally be reborn together in
the Land of Ultimate Bliss.
Homage to Amita Buddha!

NAMO AMITABHA
南 無 阿 彌 陀 佛

財 團 法 人 佛 陀 教 育 基 金 會　印 贈
台北市杭州南路一段五十五號十一樓
Printed and donated for free distribution by
The Corporate Body of the Buddha Educational Foundation
11F., 55 Hang Chow South Road Sec 1, Taipei, Taiwan, R.O.C.
Tel: 886-2-23951198 , Fax: 886-2-23913415
Email: overseas@budaedu.org
Website:http://www.budaedu.org
This book is strictly for free distribution, it is not for sale.
Printed in Taiwan
15,000 copies; April 2006
EN150-5930

....

NAME OF SPONSOR
助 印 功 德 芳 名
Document Serial No : 95051
委印文號: 95051

書　名 : Analects of Master Kuang-Ch'in (廣欽老和尚開示錄)
Book Serial No.,書號 : EN150

U.S.Dollars :
988 : 美國淨宗學會。
AMITABHA BUDDHIST SOCIETY OF U.S.A.

N.T.Dollars :
267,984 : 佛陀教育基金會。
The Corporate Body of the Buddha Educational Foundation

Amount: U.S.Dollars 988 , N.T.Dollars 267,984 , 15,000 copies.
以上合計美金 988 , 新台幣 267,984 元 , 恭印 15,000 冊。

Place to contact and order in North America :
AMITABHA BUDDHIST SOCIETY OF U.S.A.
650 S. BERNARDO AVE, SUNNYVALE, CA 94087, U.S.A.
TEL:408-736-3386　　FAX:408-736-3389
http://www.amtb-usa.org